Reflections

by

FOSTER BAILEY

Part I: Reflections

Part II: Mantrams, Ancient and Modern

LUCIS PUBLISHING COMPANY
New York

LUCIS PRESS LTD.
London

COPYRIGHT © by LUCIS TRUST

First printing 1979

The publication of this book is financed by the Lucis Trust, a tax-exempt educational corporation. The Lucis Publishing Company is a non-profit organisation owned by the Lucis Trust. No royalties are paid on this book.

MANUFACTURED IN THE UNITED STATES
By Fort Orange Press, Inc., Albany, New York

BOOKS BY FOSTER BAILEY

Changing Esoteric Values
The Spirit of Masonry
Running God's Plan
Things to Come
Reflections

BOOKS BY ALICE A. BAILEY

Initiation, Human and Solar
Letters on Occult Meditation
The Consciousness of the Atom
A Treatise on Cosmic Fire
The Light of the Soul
The Soul and Its Mechanism
From Intellect to Intuition
A Treatise on White Magic
From Bethlehem to Calvary
Discipleship in the New Age—Vol. I
Discipleship in the New Age—Vol. II
Problems of Humanity
The Reappearance of the Christ
The Destiny of the Nations
Glamour: A World Problem
Telepathy and the Etheric Vehicle
The Unfinished Autobiography
Education in the New Age
The Externalisation of the Hierarchy
A Treatise on the Seven Rays:
    Vol. I   —Esoteric Psychology
    Vol. II —Esoteric Psychology
    Vol. III—Esoteric Astrology
    Vol. IV—Esoteric Healing
    Vol. V —Rays and Initiations

CONTENTS

PART I—REFLECTIONS

PART II—MANTRAMS, ANCIENT AND MODERN

SECTION I

SECTION II

THE GREAT INVOCATION

From the point of Light within the Mind of God
Let light stream forth into the minds of men.
Let Light descend on Earth.

From the point of Love within the Heart of God
Let love stream forth into the hearts of men.
May Christ return to Earth.

From the centre where the Will of God is known
Let purpose guide the little wills of men—
The purpose which the Masters know and serve.

From the centre which we call the race of men
Let the Plan of Love and Light work out
And may it seal the door where evil dwells.

Let Light and Love and Power restore the Plan on Earth.

The above Invocation or Prayer does not belong to any person or group but to all humanity. The beauty and the strength of this Invocation lies in its simplicity, and in its expression of certain central truths which all men, innately and normally, accept—the truth of the existence of a basic Intelligence to Whom we vaguely give the name of God; the truth that behind all outer seeming, the motivating power of the universe is Love; the truth that a great Individuality came to earth, called by Christians, the Christ, and embodied that love so that we could understand; the truth that both love and intelligence are effects of what is called the Will of God; and finally the self-evident truth that only through *humanity* itself can the divine Plan work out.
                                                            —ALICE A. BAILEY

DEDICATION

This book is a posthumous publication. Foster Bailey died in 1977.

As a tribute to his life of selfless service, and in his name, *REFLECTIONS* is dedicated to all who love and serve their fellowmen.

Mary Bailey

PART I

REFLECTIONS

FOREWORD

One of the definitions of the word *reflection* given by Webster's dictionary is: "a thought, idea or remark made as a result of meditation". Reflection is so used as the title to this book. The statements made by the author may best be described as the result of meditative pondering on the problems and opportunities of world crisis. It is a mental process.

The essential required for useful results is freedom of thought. To gain this freedom, preconceived ideas and conclusions, even if good, should be temporarily set aside in considering a specific chosen event. This does not involve abandoning the concept but does include a willingness to do so if that is found wise.

A really new thought is a precious possession, a delight to savour, an expansion of consciousness and an enrichment of life. It is a joy well worth striving for. To change one's viewpoint does not belittle a man's intelligence. Indeed, to be afraid to change is unintelligent in this changing world. This changing world is the greatest day of opportunity humanity has ever had.

A second guide to useful reflection is reasonableness. Do not finally and completely reject a new thought if at first it seems unreasonable. We may think differently about it later. It is well to realise that our grasp of truth is inevitably partial and should grow as we grow. Only a few short years ago it seemed utterly unreasonable and quite silly to believe that man could walk on the surface of the moon. We need far-sighted, daring thought pioneers and a new and deeper understanding of what is really good for us as human beings.

A most useful word in considering right reflection is pondering. Pondering is a mental process which can be developed and for which there is a technique. It can, therefore, become an aid to increasing understanding and a road to wisdom. Most definitely it is not day-dreaming. Also it is not a strenuous meditation exercise requiring sustained effort. Like raja yoga and occult meditation, it does help develop mental capacity but its objective is more the achieving of understanding of a selected idea than a mind-building process. It is not a legitimate substitute for meditation.

Some people like to sit and think. For them pondering is natural. Others are too nervous, restless and impatient. For them pondering can be a health benefit, off-setting tension and nervous strain, automatically producing relaxation. Pondering requires little effort as compared to occult meditation and does not hasten one's mental evolution as much. Obviously a skilled meditator will get more out of pondering or sustained reflection than a person whose mental training has been mostly confined to memorising. Experience suggests that for the meditator, focussed reflection will be pleasant and healthful and will increase his usefulness in the practical affairs of life.

The motive power of reflection is interest in the subject and is, therefore, not a task or a discipline. It uses this interest to prolong attention.

Thus he is lined up in consciousness and the channel between his mind and brain is less impeded. This channel is spoken of as "the golden cord connecting the higher and the lower". We all have this magnetic channel and, like all else, if we know about it and let it work unhindered, it develops and becomes more useful. In meditation we focus on using it. In reflection we let it work. If we have a well-stocked mind we get new understanding.

For valuable results reflection requires the capacity to relate ideas. It goes beyond memory and analysis to analogies and conclusions which are illuminating and intriguing; our thought processes thereby become more interesting to ourselves and the ultimate result is more usefulness to those whose lives we contact.

FOSTER BAILEY

2

MODERN ESOTERICISM*

Time marches on. In 1975 the members of the spiritual Hierarchy of the planet will gather to consider what more they can do for humanity. They have more knowledge about the condition of humanity than our best informed leaders. Their focus is on the spiritual evolution of mankind as a whole. They are well aware of the fundamental law of balance operating in the life of Sanat Kumara as part of a solar process. If they overplay their hand the backlash would destroy a high percentage of any gain. How much more can they do than they are now doing? If they do too much we struggle and suffer more. And more than that, we become more dependent on them, whereas God's Plan for man is a do-it-yourself Plan.

The function of Hierarchy is to aid God's Plan which includes more than human affairs. Perhaps we think of them a little too much in terms of our own needs. Wisdom in the Hierarchy is an essential for success and in recent times they have seen to it that the second ray power they wield is complete in its manifesting, namely, in love and wisdom. Wisdom is an aspect of love in action and the coming in of seventh ray energy aids wisdom.

The present world turmoil in the minds of men brings to Hierarchy the greatest opportunity it has ever faced. This is a main significance of the present time. It is from this angle that the members of the Hierarchy confer and make decisions.

Every time the forces of darkness strike a blow and get an effect, Hierarchy under the law of balance has an opportunity to strike a blow and get an effect without danger of devastating backlash. Likewise, every time they push too hard a surge of opposing force is let loose. What they can wisely do depends on how much humanity can take.

---

* Written 1975

They are drastically limited by us. Our future is more in our hands than in theirs. As humanity matures we recognise this and accept it. If we do not recognise opportunity now we limit Hierarchy's efforts to implement God's Plan for man as well as our own self-achieved mastery of life.

We have sought to understand the reason why we are still engulfed in world crisis and have turned our attention to the action of the Hierarchy in its conclave in 1975. This we have done that we might be "doers of the word and not hearers only". We seek as best we may to be cooperators.

More than thirty years ago, Djwhal Khul wrote, "The war of 1914-1945 is over. Its aftermath of suffering, famine, selfish reactions, suspicions and unseemly struggle for supremacy is equally as bad as the past war; the effects are more lasting because the war has been largely transferred to the mental plane". These after-effects climaxed in 1975.

Students of the Ancient Wisdom realise that the human family as a whole has continued to live by wrong life values, the results of which have produced a final character test of the whole human race. We recall that D.K. said that two generations would determine whether material or spiritual values would dominate human life for long years to come. The struggle between the forces of light and the forces of darkness was not ended in 1942.

What can we do? What is practically possible? Certain factors emerge, based upon our group experience, particularly in the last twenty years. We know that the heart of humanity is sound. We know that the total effectiveness of hierarchical effort to help humanity has increased. We know that the constructive influence of the Aquarian age is stronger than the habit momentum of the Piscean age. We know that the persisting action of Hierarchy to make the energy of goodwill abundantly available has prevented crisis after crisis in world affairs from producing a third world war. We know that humanity has matured amazingly in the last generation and is now capable of controlling its own destiny. We know that spiritual potency is stronger than the influence of heartless greed because so many of us have become more aware of world affairs than ever before. We know that the men and women of good-will are more active than ever before, and that the use of the Great Invocation is more worldwide and more potent.

Perhaps more important than all the above factors is the increased realisation that we individually share respon-sibility. We have tended to feel entitled to leaders whom we could idealise and follow. We have in the past, as chil-dren, wanted to be saved more than we have wanted to save ourselves, but we have been maturing spiritually very rapidly.

World Crisis

There are two aspects to the present worldwide crisis as to its causes. One is the accumulated results of living by wrong values, forcing change, and the other is the mental growth of humanity itself; justifying a greatly increased personal responsibility for the future of humanity as a whole.

New understanding of what affects humanity as a whole is emerging and the will to face up to it is increasing. These two factors are of more importance than specific reforms of established procedures. One of the most essential needs for the future well-being of all of us is the activating of the millions of men and women of goodwill to accept responsi-bility for world conditions.

This maturing of human responsibility for human destiny requires a more wise use of thought power in a broader field than ever before. It necessitates identifying better values to live by plus action to put them into effect.

The majority of the people in the human family need even minimum necessities for a decent life. It is not what they want but what they must have. For the rest of us it is what we want, not necessities. If we want wrong things we degrade ourselves. Those in dire need are helpless. We are not. Those who have almost nothing to live on cannot degrade themselves much more. We can.

In the affluent countries there are small minorities who

still need necessities and this is an obvious shame in the midst of plenty. Also, there are minority groups in the rich nations who do not get justice. Perhaps justice should come second to life necessities in our understanding of right values. The peoples who have enough money to provide unnecessary indulgences and a soft life want more. It in fact amounts to class greed. Perhaps sharing instead of grasping is a value to live by of equal importance to justice. Those who have abundance are the best educated, which, no matter how much we shrink from it, brings responsibility. Those who have are responsible for world misery of millions and their indifference only postpones the day of reckoning. Responsibility for the common good is as important a value to live by as any. Competition between the strong has resulted in two percent of the people of the, just now, for a time, wealthiest nation in the world owning 90 percent of the wealth. This lopsided imbalance is eloquent of the need of a better value to live by. The value of cooperation should be very high on our list of better values. Misuse of power, particularly in government and business, has produced many rebellions and still does. Right use of power should also come high in our recognition of better values to live by. And there are many more better values which unselfish, clear thinking reveals.

We should not shrink from identifying right values to live by, and when so identified they do not have to be implemented one at a time. The will to better world conditions and the better life for all is supported by the fact that we are one family and can and should live as one family. Brotherhood is real and universal and inevitably it will manifest as the most basic fact of human life. Shall we say that brotherhood is the most important value to live by of them all?

There are manifest differences in various segments of the human family due to many causes, some very ancient. There are also various human qualities common to all in differing degree. Behind it all is the fact that all humanity had a common source, has a common goal, and that there is an overall Plan for man.

"God hath made all men of the same blood". The blood of a coloured man can be used in a blood transfusion into a white man with no detriment to the white man, and *vice versa*. What we indicate by the word brotherhood is a reality existing today, however it is violated and however much it is ignored. The glamour that we are not all one family under God has brought all of us at this time of the end of the age to maximum world turmoil and crisis. This greatest heresy of separateness is the basic cause of present conditions. It is a heresy not against a church or an ideology but against the divine Plan for man and the very reason why there is such a thing as humanity at all.

In *Problems of Humanity*, pages 87-9, we read that there is no greater sin than separateness. Here D.K. tells us that separateness is responible for the entire range of human evil. He says: "It sets an individual against his brother; it makes him consider his selfish, personal interests as of paramount importance; it leads inevitably to crime and cruelty; it constitutes the greatest hindrance to happiness in the world, for it sets man against man, group against group, class against class and nation against nation. It engenders a destructive sense of superiority and leads to the pernicious doctrine of superior and inferior nations and races; it produces economic selfishness and leads to the economic exploitation of human beings, to trade barriers, to the condition of have and have-not, to territorial possessiveness and to the extremes of poverty and riches; it sets an important emphasis upon material acquisitiveness, upon boundaries, and the dangerous doctrine of national sovereignty with its various selfish implications; it breeds distrust between peoples and hatred throughout the entire world and has led since time began to cruel and destructive wars. It has today brought the entire planetary population to its present dire and dreadful condition so that men everywhere are beginning to realise that unless something is fundamentally changed, mankind is practically already destroyed. But who will engineer the needed change and where is the leadership which will bring it about? It is a state of affairs which mankind itself must face as a whole; and by meeting and facing this basic expression of universal wrongdoing, humanity can bring about the needed change and is offered a new opportunity for right action, leading to right human relations".

D.K. goes on to speak of the spirit of nationalism with its insistence on sovereignty. This is a substitute for the old age monarchy and rule by armed conquest and is the basis of modern dictatorships. It has been truly said that there is a little of the totalitarian in all of us. D.K. says: "This, in its worst aspect, sets one nation against another, fosters a sense of national superiority and leads the citizens of a nation to regard themselves and their institutions as superior to those of another nation; it cultivates pride of race, of history, of possessions, and of cultural progress and breeds an arrogance, a boastfulness and a contempt of other civilisations and cultures which is evil and degenerating; it engenders also a willingness to sacrifice other people's interests to one's own and a basic failure to admit that 'God hath made all men equal'. This type of nationalism is universal and everywhere to be found and no nation is free from it; it indicates a blindness, a cruelty and a lack of proportion for which mankind is already paying a terrible price and which will bring humanity down in ruins if persisted in.

"There is, needless to say, an ideal nationalism which is the reverse of all this; it exists as yet only in the minds of an enlightened few in every nation, but it is not yet an effective and constructive aspect of any nation anywhere; it remains still a dream, a hope and, let us believe, a fixed intention. This type of nationalism rightly fosters its individual civilisation but as a national contribution to the general good of the comity of nations and not as a means of self-glorification; it defends its constitution, its lands and its people through the rectitude of its living expression, the beauty of its mode of life and the selflessness of its attitudes;

it does not infringe, for any reason, the rights of other people or nations. It aims to improve and perfect its own mode of life so that all in the world may benefit. It is a living, vital, spiritual organism and not a selfish, material organisation".

Much of the wrong functioning of our civilisation in domestic affairs arises out of the anarchy in the international world of sovereign states because scientific achievement has brought us to worldwide interdependence. Just as the people of a small village have to cooperate for the good of the village or explode into fragments, so nations will in the long last give up some of their sovereignty for world welfare for all mankind. Already in a few limited cases a real beginning has been made. World unity is a possibility and is a definite project of the spiritual Hierarchy of the planet today.

Vehicles for the Soul

Evolution is a process of growth. So far as humanity is concerned on this planet there is growth of the form to be used by the life and growth in consciousness. This results in growth of the manifestation of life. Growth appears to characterise everything in this solar system and also at least in that part of the cosmos in which our solar system finds its place. We know nothing to negate the idea that growth is a fundamental, universal fact in the entire cosmos.

That portion of manifesting life we call the soul is the result of a certain type of life using an appropriate type of substance as a vehicle of self-expression. Given the basic premise of the reality of growth, that is a reasonable concept, and with our present stage of growth in consciousness that is about as far as we can go. Assuredly what little we comprehend about it is only a tiny bit of the entire reality and we would be foolish indeed to be dogmatic about it.

We do know something about mental, emotional and physical substance and have achieved by means of growth, or evolution, some individual consciousness in relation to those three kinds of matter. This the divine life in us has achieved by appropriating a portion of these three grades of substance to use for our own destiny. That bit of substance we are using we call our bodies and we have mental and emotional bodies as well as a physical body.

What we call immortality is the conscious use of our emotional and mental bodies after we have stopped our use of a physical body and the soul is what is meant by that word "we". Using our birthright of mental freedom, we go beyond even that in our mental venturing to a spiritual life unit called by esoteric pioneers the monad, positing the idea that the relation of the soul to the monad is at least somewhat like the relation of the personality to the human soul. Again it would be foolish to be dogmatic.

We can be quite reasonable in accepting the idea that all manifested life is interrelated and that all manifesting life has the ability to pass on that life into new bodies of various grades of substance. The process of getting a new physical body in the human kingdom on this planet is an example. The same creative aspect of our souls must manifest in taking emotional and mental bodies although the details may well be quite different and at present unknown to us. We develop our mental consciousness by daring to ponder the unknown. If we did not venture into the unknown, human evolution might stop.

On the physical plane we know that the birth process has a sequential time schedule. We know that without the limitation of a physical brain, time is transcended in consciousness to a considerable degree at least. For this reality we have already some partial evidence accepted by many rational intellectuals but still considered unproven by many. Also there is reason to believe that what we call being tired is a condition of our physical bodies but not of our emotional or mental bodies. Ill health is a condition of the matter of our physical bodies but apparently not of our emotional or mental bodies, although under the law of analogy there may well be some process in the emotional and mental bodies analogous to growing old. There are surely limitations inherent in all grades of substance as compared to soul consciousness.

According to all the ancient as well as modern esoteric teachings all substance of every plane has seven differentiated subdivisions, and the physical substance of our solar system is the most dense of the seven grades of cosmic substance. If this be so, the vehicle our soul uses on its own plane is a subplane of the cosmic physical plane.

That all substance on all planes affects substance on every other plane would seem certain because all substance has life in common. Every doctor knows that the emotional condition of his patient affects his physical body condition and every student of psychology knows the emotional condition and habits affect the mind, even in extremes to insanity. Also, all life, in whatever stage of manifestation, affects all life on the plane of the soul and by analogy all the planes of substance in our solar life expression. This is the basis of the teaching that the illusion of separateness is the greatest heresy. All life in our solar system is the manifestation of the one total life in the system and, as a unit, is a part of the life of a greater life unit in cosmos.

The proper function of our solar life must be adjusted to other solar lives in what we might call right solar relations, just as all the parts of the life of the human kingdom require right human relations. To consider that all the little units in the human kingdom are in competition with all other human units is utterly unreasonable. Cooperation in action implemented by a loving heart is only commonsense. The new age teaching about life must be reasonable or it will not take hold.

The home of the human soul is on the mental plane. This plane consists of substance of the fifth subplane of the cosmic physical plane, counting from the most subtle substance down to the more dense. As may well be supposed, the denser the substance the more limitation there is to the life aspect using it and it is this fact which is the basis of the ancient dictum that "the mind is the slayer of the real". This is quite so as to human consciousness at our present stage of evolution, but as the life increasingly controls the forms it uses it will be less and less the case.

The Evolution of Consciousness

The position of organised religion is that we still as mental children should be controlled by authority and that religious dogmas do not have to be reasonable. This they call religious faith and by it man is said to be rightly controlled by a power outside himself.

As man matures and the mind is further developed we will be controlled increasingly from within ourselves by the power of the life more fully controlling our minds, interpreted and accepted according to its reasonableness. The coming new religion in the Aquarian age will be reasonable. In the Piscean age the form has too much controlled the life. In the Aquarian age the life will more adequately control the form.

The pressing question confronting all of us in this climaxing world crisis is: where does humanity go from here? Can we set a goal for human life on this planet? Can we in fact do anything about it? Such questions have ceased to be philosophical intellectualisations.

Some basic concepts are increasingly accepted by intelligent people all over the world. Among them we may include:

1. Evolution is a fact. Humanity is evolving.
2. The goal of human evolution is expansion of consciousness.
3. Increased consciousness requires mental development.
4. The most important leadership is thought leadership.
5. The most important aid is education.

To be effective education must have right goals. The present educational systems lack vision as to what results education should produce. The present stage of human evolution has produced analytical, critical, selfish, materialistic thinking. This has been inevitable because mental capacity gets individuals what they want. Many accept economic progress as the most important life factor. We have taught our students to be self-reliant and to get whatever they want if they can, and have produced a civilisation which is breaking down all around us. Planetary conditions now compel us to face it.

Individual greed gets short-term results if aggressive enough but requires indifference to the misery of millions of people. Success in competition goes to the powerful. Those who now have can get more. Those who have almost nothing can get nothing more unless the goal of the common good for all men supersedes the goal of individual good, so called, which turns out to be not so good after all. What we have called a successful life is a degrading life.

To consider that man is nothing but a physical body and that when he loses that body that is the end of him, is childish ignorance. To consider that there are no human powers and realities beyond what science can now prove to its own satisfaction is a denial of most of life itself. To accept science as an authority of what human evolution is all about is to forfeit our birthright. Science has brought tremendous new knowledge and marvelous new power over nature to mankind. Its achievements are the first stage in humanity's mental evolution. We have made it the servant of wrong values and submit too much to its powerful influence. The trouble is more with us than with science and it is our wrong life values that have led many scientists to over-glorify their profession.

But the evolution of consciousness goes on and life itself is more wonderful than we have yet conceived. The newly recognised technique in the West for expanding our consciousness is meditation, a science without test tubes. The science of meditation is very old in the East, particularly in India, and takes many forms, but its use has almost entirely been promoted for individual gain. Eastern imports of meditation are not enough. We need a threefold approach of meditation, study and service to others. Meditation for personal gain can enable us to register more phenomena but can be misused in exactly the same way that we have misused science. The meditation technique is so powerful when somewhat mastered that its abuse can accelerate the degeneration of our civilisation. Meditation for selfish, greedy purposes is as destructive as any other selfish, greedy purpose. More mental power is dangerous to ourselves unless it is accompanied by a new and deeper acceptance of responsibility for the good of others. Usefulness to others is the best safeguard against self-destruction that we have. This necessitates the development of the heart quality along with mental power and this heart quality in expression substitutes cooperation for competition, sharing for grasping, and honesty for deceit.

What is Love?

Generally speaking most people consider love as an emotion. To them, love of one's friends is a diluted form of love. Parental love is stronger, natural and praiseworthy. Love's most potent form is sexual. When given right expression it produces joy and even ecstacy. A loveless life is a barren life. Love is such a potent emotion that it often over-rides reason and ignores future results. In its most perfect manifestation it produces kindness and sacrifice for the loved one. Justice, patience, forgiveness, truthfulness blossom in its light. It cannot be purchased by money or gained by flattery. True love spontaneously desires to be useful to the one loved.

Christ revealed love two thousand years ago. Our Christian bible describes love beautifully. "Though I speak with the tongues of men and of angels but have not love, I am become as sounding brass or a tinkling cymbal. And though I have the gift of prophecy and understand all mysteries, and all knowledge; and though I have all faith so that I could remove mountains and have not love, I am nothing. And though I bestow all my goods to feed the poor, and though I give my body to be burned, and have not love, it profiteth me nothing. Love suffereth long and is kind; love envieth not; love vaunteth not itself, is not puffed up, doth not behave itself unseemly, seeketh not her own, is not easily provoked, thinketh no evil, rejoiceth not in iniquity, but rejoiceth in the truth. Beareth all things, believeth all things, hopeth all things, endureth all things. Love never faileth". Love has been proclaimed through the years as the greatest thing in the world.

But love is also a mental energy as well as an emotion, and its mental qualities add to its value and make it even more real. It will profit us much to think deeply about love.

Djwhal Khul tells us that "love is essentially a word for the underlying motive of creation". From these few words great truth emerges. We expand our consciousness when we persistently ask why, and expanding consciousness is a goal of human evolution itself. Why is there a type of life on this planet Earth which we call the human kingdom? As a child-race we were told that we could know nothing about such things but now that humanity has come of age we are discovering that we can. Let us welcome our adulthood.

Love reveals the reason for all creation. Its mental expression therefore transcends its emotional registration. It holds hid the key of why man is. It is the one great essential for right human relations. A spontaneous result of loving relations produces cooperation and sharing and makes world unity possible. It is the essence of brotherhood and all men are spiritual brothers. Brotherhood is a fact in nature which we have smothered in our ignorance and greed and our slavery to the great heresy of separateness.

We place the seat of love in the heart and recognise that the heart circulates the blood and that the blood is the life. When the heart stops, physical life ends, and it may therefore be said that love makes life possible. In this present moral world crisis with its confusion and suffering, the one factor most needed by all humanity is love and its most acceptable expression is goodwill, which is rightly defined as love-in-action.

Our esoteric studies have told us that the present solar system in which our planet Earth now functions, is the second in a series of three, and that the basic divine energy wielded by our solar Logos is love. The great centre of purpose, Shamballa, "where the will of God is known," exists to energise the heart of God which on the planet is focussed in the spiritual Hierarchy, presided over by the great world executive called by Christians, the Christ. This Hierarchy is an energy centre of love.

So also is the new group of world servers. This new group is an energy channel carrying the quality of the Hierarchy and of the Christ into the hearts and minds of humanity as a whole. It is love that unites and holds all the planets in our solar system in one united expression of divine life and makes it possible for our solar Logos to express His essential divine life in relation to other solar systems.

Servers with the Christ

Increasingly as we escape from our self-centredness we can join the ranks of all true world servers. The door is open to us and no one can stop us but ourselves. We do not have to join any exoteric organisation or submit to any imposed authority. We do not have to accept or follow any leader. We do not have to tell anybody. We remain completely free and in control of our own destiny. And with it all, we find a new joyousness in being a human being and escape from fear and futility. This we do as soul-infused personalities. We can then join the new group of world servers. Such a joining is legitimate if we want humanity to be helped more than we want to be the helpers of humanity.

We need not delay. We can begin at once. We can help channel spiritual energy into humanity as a pulsation of light carrying light and love and spiritual power to all men everywhere in the world. Petty personal problems then disappear and we know at last what real freedom is.

We have much knowledge of the spiritual Hierarchy of the planet and in recent days much new teaching about Shamballa, the centre where the Will of God is known. Using the mind, we can link up with the world ashram of Sanat Kumara and begin to become world conscious and planetary citizens. So under God's Plan for man we become adults. We graduate from being followers of the Christ and become cooperators with the Christ, at first in a very limited way, but once having begun, increasing in usefulness to him. He aids humanity and so can we. The world is at crisis and we can help.

New Age Esotericism

An intelligent entry by the human family into the new Aquarian age requires a blending of the eastern and western approaches to life. In this new age hundreds of thousands of men of goodwill can achieve a degree of planetary consciousness never before possible and many will achieve an identification with humanity as a whole which will produce a planetary citizenship which will include national citizenship and racial relations adjusted to a greater good for all men.

An outstanding characteristic of eastern culture is its many systems of yoga. Yogic practices are no longer considered freakish in the West and are increasingly used, often with most inadequate instruction, lack of understanding, and they are inaccurate in many details. The misuse of yoga in the West may well subvert a needed new age blending of eastern and western understanding of right life values. Yoga should be understood not condemned. Assuming a posture, reciting magic mantrams, breathing exercises, blanking the mind, etc., all with selfish motive, can delay personal evolution and are not of themselves spiritual. Used for personality aggrandisement they are delaying side-tracks to expansion of spiritual progress. Some caution and warning about yoga in the West is needed but this eastern teaching brings a new and needed technique in mind control for spiritual purposes.

The most useful yoga for the westerner is available to us in the *yoga sutras* of Patanjali. This yoga has been called *Raja Yoga, the Kingly Science of Union*. It requires a positively controlled mental effort and transcends mystical experiences. Modern western esotericism trains the mind to become the instrument of the soul. The preliminary stages are not easy and require persistence. For best results it should be a daily practice with accompanying study of spiritual teachings and an increasing life activity of usefulness to others. It is an applied philosophy of life.

Most of the yogas now extant will not increase in usefulness in the new Aquarian age and will, therefore, die out. This is also true of Piscean age religions now in decline.

The last few years of the Piscean era, more particularly the last two hundred, saw the birth of esoteric schools in the West. They could not be called popular in relation to the somewhat mental types of men of goodwill but they were at least open to the populace. That is to say they were not secret schools and many of them blatantly advertised their wares, and still do.

Speaking generally, the attracting bait varied from the crudest forms of psychic powers, for so many lessons at a fixed price, to disciplines for personal progress on the evolutionary path. The disciplines were imposed by the school joined and a considerable degree of obedience about things considered essential was exacted. These essentials were often not thought of as spiritual. Although in many cases meetings were private and sometimes passwords used, and although the lesson papers were never to be shared with outsiders, it was not difficult to find and join most of these groups. Unlike the secret esoteric groups of the middle ages no penalties and no dire punishments were set up, save only the threat of possible expulsion.

With the coming of H. P. Blavatsky and the publishing of her teaching and that of her second generation followers, most of the material used as study in these latter day schools gradually became available to all. This process was climaxed by Alice A. Bailey's work with the Tibetan and the publication of *Discipleship in the New Age*. With the exoteric mystery removed from the "Schools of the Mysteries" it remained, therefore, for the authoritative schools only to keep the faithful properly lined up in obedience to such esoteric standards, if any, as the teacher chose to demand.

Any effective practice of meditation has been, for the most part, more emotional than mental although not so recognised, and much more mystical than occult. Prior to 1923 the uniqueness necessary to attract the aspirant was essentially an importation from the East of bhakti yoga, with a tinge of laya yoga, and in the more venturesome and crude groups an admixture of hatha yoga. Raja yoga, a definitely mental yoga, was sometimes touched but in reality little practiced. Even in the best of the schools physical disciplines, such as vegetarianism, were considered more important than mental discipline and regular systematic study with required written work was a rare exception. Where written work was used, it was patterned after secular education in that it was a matter of learning what was presented to the student more than reasoning about what was taught, much less any application to the spiritual problems confronting humanity in the modern world.

At this stage of the introduction of esotericism to the West true self-reliance in the aspirant was rare. There was a necessity for a leader who could be idealised and for an outside authority accepted because of that trusted leader. If this would-be leader did not have the needed kudos in his own right, he had perforce to proclaim his potency to lead on the basis of having been trained by some superior leader. Gradually, therefore, the spiritual progress of the student becomes imperceptibly secondary to the perpetuation of the leadership, which is apt to be justified as the perpetuation of "the teaching". It is obviously easier to have a larger school if the students who do not want to work do not have to.

Notwithstanding any and all defects in the esoteric field, the close of the Piscean era sees a most successful operation upon the expanding consciousness of western civilisation by the Hierarchy using, as perforce they must, the best disciples they could get for the arduous task required. The implanting of some esoteric knowledge free to all in the western world was an hierarchical project of long-range vision and profound spiritual importance for the new era.

During the last hundred years the type of esoteric training made available was primarily at the probationary path level and this was necessarily so. Out of this training here and there a disciple emerged worthy to enter a Master's ashram and to take initiation. This then became the shining goal, the great achievement and the inciting factor necessary for perseverance. Speculation as to who had taken what initiation was the gossip of the groups. Personal progress on the path was the driving force in the life of the aspirant.

Clearly something needed to be done to break this spiritually selfish motivation, and under impression from the Hierarchy, esoteric leaders began to stress *service*. First service to the leader, then service to the school one had joined, then service by way of propaganda for selected doctrines such as reincarnation, and finally service to the Plan. Meanwhile, Christianity was producing the few who served their fellowmen solely for the sake of those served, and the esoteric schools also produced a few. These are the real new age disciples whether in or outside of the esoteric field.

On the probationary path there were valiant attempts to "serve the Master", and much sacrificing work to spread "the truth" with persistent effort to get ahead spiritually. These motives are praiseworthy and have borne much fruit in preparing the esoteric field for its graduation into the new day. It has laid the foundation for what is possible to us now. All honour then to the leaders in this work and just recognition of what they have achieved. Also it is to be remembered that in our modern times there will be many thousands who will profitably enter probationary path training as compared with the pioneering hundreds ready to attempt discipleship. The probationary path remains essential to the great ladder of evolution as is the general mental progress of the race, as also indeed is the more exacting path of discipleship which follows thereon.

A percentage of those who achieve some real capacity to live and work at the discipleship level will, and should, find useful service in the probationary path field. At this level a new and more highly motivated school is now needed.

Here and there a few will qualify to teach and lead in the as yet so little understood curriculum of new age pioneering world discipleship training.

The large majority who attain to discipleship usefulness to the Plan, to the Hierarchy and to their fellowmen, will find their sphere of action in the ranks of the new group of world servers in its seven major departments. This goal, therefore, should be the *major interest* and effort of the modern esoteric schools for discipleship if they are to fulfill their rightful destiny and demonstrate their most essential usefulness. A discipleship school not contributing to the success of the new group of world servers is abortive. The Master Djwhal Khul has stated that in the new age the field of training for the disciple is in the new group of world servers.

Recognising the still limited vision we as yet have of the new Aquarian way of life, what can now be said as to the immediate practical points of emphasis most likely to bring the spiritual results which are possible to us?

First. The new age discipleship schools must achieve deeper vision as to spiritual values. This vision comes into the brain consciousness via the soul. It is not a product of the mind. It is best achieved by group invocation using "the science of group impression". To achieve this group invocative power, the *need* must be clearly recognised. The Master has said: "Changes mean nothing unless they are the result of *new vision,* for if they emerge out of criticism of the past and of what has been done they will prove useless from the angle of the spiritual life, no matter how useful they may be from the angle of the organisation". He has also admonished us to "keep the work fluid" *for change we must.*

Second. The training should orient the student more definitely to discipleship *living* than heretofore. This means a more keen purpose of the would-be disciple to be *useful* to the Hierarchy. This usefulness is the crux of the rate of progress in every ashram from the periphery towards the centre. To desire to be useful is more essential than to desire progress on the path. We recall that A.A.B. challenged the headquarters group in the Arcane School only a few months before she died, asking them, "How can we change the Arcane School from a group of students into a group that the Hierarchy can more effectively use?"

Third. The motivating drive must be lifted as nearly to the level of the Hierarchy as can be achieved. The deepest, most impelling motive of the Hierarchy is service of humanity. To this end they strive to implement the Plan because the Plan itself is a Plan *for humanity.*

Fourth. A discipleship school should attract those students who are at the end of the probationary path, and who can, with the aid of the spiritual stimulant of the school group, take the crucial step of attempting more rapid progress than is normal to the probationary path, and so move on to the discipleship path. This is done under influence and pressure from their own souls. If it is a personality motivated step because of intellectual interest, spiritual ambition, or other probationary path motives, it is not strong enough to take the strain. In that case, if the spiritual quality of the school is right and of discipleship status, the result is a non-working member or a drop-out. In an effort to prevent the Arcane School from becoming a probationary path school after her passing, A.A.B. abandoned the first two degrees and stated that we should not continue to have non-working members.

Fifth. The keynote of the individual aspirant to discipleship must be more *impersonal* and *selfless* than heretofore. This must be relentlessly promoted, although aspirants on the probationary path find this quality cold and, therefore, fall away. To these two qualities must be increasingly demonstrated the sense of *responsibility*, of *sacrifice* and of *comradeship*. In recent times a Master has said to his chela:

"1. The sense of responsibility shines forth in flickering flames from every soul which has sought and found alignment. Fan those flames into a steady fire in every soul you meet.

2. The sense of sacrifice is faintly seen in every soul that loves the Plan. Teach them that sacrifice must touch the depths of giving and not call forth that which upon the surface lies or that which can be known. The unseen sacrifice must go with that which can be seen. Teach this.

3. The sense of comradeship is surely known by each and all of you but needs the deepening of service shared. Show this and draw it forth. The comradeship of burdens shared, the sense of deep response to need, the comradeship of service rendered, the urge to sacrifice—teach these to those who seek to work within the Master's plan and show all three yourself".

These five qualities with the resulting strength of *joy* will carry the disciple far.

Sixth. To the continuing study of spiritual teachings, which eventually are self-chosen, and control of the mind through meditation, which practice continues to the very end, there must be added knowledge of world problems in relation to spiritual values and hierarchical purpose and *training in service.*

"The ancient activities of the Hierarchy will still persist, including the activities of preparing disciples and initiates for initiation and for participating consciously in hierarchical effort. The Schools of the Mysteries [as outlined in *Letters on Occult Meditation*] will come into being but this will be temporarily a secondary activity. The full expression of ashramic energy will be directed to practical world affairs and to the education of the general public, and not in the early stages to esoteric matters".

Here we have an almost inevitable struggle between those who sincerely idealise the teacher-pupil relationship and those who are more willing to trust the developed soul-control of membership. That the pupil should ultimately not need the teacher guidance, so essential at an earlier stage, is intellectually accepted but in practice is often delayed as long as possible.

The key to the successful new esoteric discipleship schools lies in the achieving of this sixth point. And this in turn will require success in the first point else we discover that for us also the mind can become "the slayer of the real". The achievement of this sixth point does not require belittlement, much less abandonment, of continued study and meditation. Indeed study and meditation are essential to its success. But, says the Tibetan, "You will all awaken someday to the realisation that the Science of Service is of greater importance than the Science of Meditation, because it is the effort and the strenuous activity of the serving disciple which evokes all the soul powers, makes meditation an essential requirement and is the mode—ahead of all others —which invokes the spiritual triad, brings about the intensification of the spiritual life, forces the building of the Antahkarana, and leads in a graded series of renunciations to the great renunciation which sets the disciple free for all eternity".

Training in cooperation with the Hierarchy in serving the Plan to solve human world problems is our hard task. This requires greater effort than any group has as yet put into it. It requires a new and deeper understanding than we now have of what is going on in the world. It requires a newborn capacity to see the emerging spiritual values in spite of blatant human errors. It necessitates an application of spiritual principles to world affairs. It must include effective cooperation with the world disciples who are today carrying the load of leadership in human progress and who have little knowledge, or none at all, of esoteric teaching. In terms more familiar to us all, it means the achieving of a soul-infused life here and now.

To successfully carry forward Aquarian discipleship the *will-to-love* and the *will-to-serve* must be strenuously evoked.

"*Love* is response to contact. This in the human being means understanding, inclusiveness and identification.

Wisdom connotes skill in action as the result of developed love and the light of understanding; it is awareness of requirements and ability to bring together into a fused relationship the need and that which will meet it.

Service is essentially a scientific mode of expressing love-wisdom under the influence of one or other of the seven rays, according to the soul ray of the serving disciple".

New Age Teaching

We now have twenty-four books giving us the teaching needed for the present interim period. They contain statements appropriate to this cycle and its production was an accepted task of the Master Djwhal Khul on behalf of the Hierarchy. The first phase was carried out with the aid of H. P. Blavatsky, the second with the aid of Alice A. Bailey, and the third will make use of the radio and television. In the first part of D.K.'s work with A.A.B., she acted as his amanuensis; in the last few years she was more of an assisting cooperator.

When working with H.P.B. in producing *The Secret Doctrine*, D.K. promised to give out at a later date the psychological key to *The Secret Doctrine*, and this he did in *A Treatise on Cosmic Fire*, published in 1925. This is his major contribution to the expanding revelation of esoteric teaching. It is a book of 1,283 pages of text with thirteen charts and seven full-page tabulations, and an index.

D.K.'s teaching includes many occult affirmations and words of power. Certain words and mantra have a potency within themselves which when correctly used release spiritual energy. They are "words of power". Hierarchy uses them and humanity is beginning to use them with intelligent purpose.

In the first part of the book, *A Treatise on Cosmic Fire,* we are given thirteen Stanzas of Dzyan and at the end, seven stanzas from the book of Archaic Formulas. D.K. says that these formulas are from the oldest book in the world and that he has given us not translations but a paraphrase in the English language as he did for the *yoga sutras* of Patanjali. He has also given us extracts from the "Old Commentary" and from the Archives of the Lodge of Masters. In *Initiation, Human and Solar,* we find Archive XIII of these records of the Masters (pp 209-213).

The giving out of the Great Invocation is the greatest and most astounding event in all D.K.'s work for us as a teacher. He brought it through in English, and it has been translated into some one hundred languages and dialects and is used all over the world by individuals and groups. Its effect is as a word of power, carrying its own inherent spiritual potency. There is now no hour in the twenty-four hours of a day when it is not in use somewhere. Its invocative sound goes out constantly and it is well on the way to becoming a new age world prayer. The Masters of the Wisdom in the Hierarchy use it as also does the Christ, but in a slightly different form.

The Mantram of Unification [page 126], beginning with the well-known words, "The sons of men are one and I am one with them", is a mantric statement second only to the Great Invocation itself. This entire affirmation acts as a word of power and contains individual words of power as well. We also have the mantric statement giving the qualities of occult world servers in the new group of world servers, which itself is a word of power. We also have the declaration of the applicant to the third major planetary initiation, as well as many other statements containing words of power.

Mystical meditation uses the mind very little and through desire and high aspiration achieves dominance of the higher subplanes of the emotional plane. It is focussed on emotional values registered in the brain and in extreme success the devotee loses consciousness. It ignores the divine part of man, the soul, and focusses on divinity *outside* of man.

Occult meditation achieves success by conscious, planned control of the mind. It has a self-chosen goal and the whole personality controls all three vehicles—mental, emotional and physical. It seeks awareness of the divine *in* man in terms of soul control and soul consciousness. This is achieved by prolonged effort on the part of the entire man, based upon a self-chosen specific purpose. The first stage is concentrated attention on a seed thought which produces a quieting of the mind in a positive condition, holding it steady in the light of the soul all through the meditation process. This is a mastery of the lower mind at the insistence of the entire man. It produces the stabilisation of the emotional vehicle and gets emotional energies out of the way. It requires relaxation but not a negative condition of the physical body. To whatever extent occult meditation is successful, the soul then controls the whole man as one unit.

Words of power and mantrams are useful in mystical meditation operating automatically on faith. They affect the meditating man by virtue of their own inherent potency irrespective of what the meditator does. The power derives from the fact that they are permutations of the sacred word of the fifth root race, the AUM. This facilitates the goal of the fifth root race (the present root race) in terms of human consciousness. This fifth root race word carries long-range, divinely created power, not originating in human evolution but a gift of God, so to speak.

There is a technique of conscious use of words of power which is different from their use in occult meditation and follows naturally after the last stage of occult meditation called contemplation. This technique calls for no mental effort and gets the lower mind out of the way just as occult meditation gets the emotions out of the way, and it is also utterly different from mystical meditation. It is possible after mind control has become something of a habit. Its use is indicated in the rules for applicants for the first initiation. This rule is: "When application has been made in triple form let the disciple withdraw that application and forget it has been made". This action leaves the words of power unmodified by the lower mind with resulting freedom of manifestation in their own right and with a human sounding board provided.

The stages arc:

1. Recognition of value in selected words of power and mantrams.
2. Careful correct sounding of them.
3. Thinking clearly of their significance long enough to build a thoughtform.
4. Stopping mental action in relation to them.
5. Forgetting that they have been invoked, with complete confidence in the results of their power.
6. A quiet waiting for an inevitable mental registering, arising not from individual desire and free from personal motives.
7. When the impulse comes to recall his invocation, let the disciple do so, not insistently but always confidently at ease. If the response does not come, put the whole thing aside and start all over again.

The technique used in gaining the effectiveness of words of power can also be used to increase the effectiveness of the soul in its increasing dominance of the personality. This effectiveness depends upon a degree of receptivity of that part of the substance of the mental plane being used by the personality. The focus is on the soul, and success entails discipleship status. It also results from the increased interest of the soul in the incarnated man which, before discipleship, has been partial. This means that the soul is really on the job.

The advancing disciple learns in due course to identify three vibrations in his brain mechanism: that of his soul, that of his ashram with which he is magnetically linked and that of the Master at the head of that ashram. The longing to get in contact with his Master has been a major motivation for spiritual exercises and meditation and has been very personal in the prior stages of spiritual unfoldment, but at this stage of evolution the disciple has come to be less personal and more knowledgeable about the quality of the Master and of the purposes activating the ashram. Personality focus blocks the development of the later stages and when this dies out the sensitivity of the disciple's response to Hierarchy is increased. The Master and his ashram are integrated parts of the Hierarchy and the relationship sought is enlarged to the Hierarchy as a whole and so to the head of Hierarchy, for in a real sense the Hierarchy is the ashram of the Christ. The vibration of the Hierarchy is more potent than that of any single Master and eventually the disciple is able to know when he is tuned in to Hierarchy.

D.K. has given us a hint on how to get right spiritual information and right answers to discipleship problems, by three stages of mental attention.

1. Link up with your soul.
2. Link up with your ashram.
3. Link up with your Master. (In that order).

This we can do by strong focussed purpose.

When application by the personality to get soul knowledge has been duly made, then let the disciple put aside all thought about it and ignore the fact that application has been made. Then the soul is more free and the effect of the power of the soul, as in the case of the effect of words of power, is more definite. Thus an effect of soul contact emerges in the consciousness of the disciple and right attitude and action are possible. If this new understanding, always characterised by increased conviction of rightness, does not come, simply start the process of this technique all over again happily and with no sense of personal failure and no impatience. The effort must be to get a soul answer, not an answer delighting the personality.

Selflessness is the key to the success of the whole process. This characterises the truly effective members of the new group of world servers and is an essential part of necessary purification before initiation.

Right Use of the Mind

The power of thought is tremendous. This we know and seek to use for the common good. Group meditation is the most potent way yet developed of using this thought energy. The practice of group meditation is increasing all over the world as never before.

With this background and powerful influence we can press on to greater usefulness of our individual thought in daily expression. Our thought life is more important than our daily action. At first blush this may seem exaggerated and a bit unreasonable, but it is not so. What my thought is mostly focussed upon all day every day has a far greater effect on what sort of a person I am than any other one factor in my life. We are not half using the potential of our thought power and are held down by our thought habits. The ultimate essential contribution of the human family to God's Plan for man during this world cycle is spiritually-controlled thought. In this we seek to participate.

It is the function of the human kingdom on this planet to develop the mind. It is the ability to think which is humanity's unique contribution to the entire planetary process. Therefore, it is clear that our thought life is of transcending importance. If it does not express our soul life purpose we fail. If it does not carry the quality of love we are selling our birthright.

Out of each day's working consciousness, how much time do we use in thought? Do we think as much as we think we think? Or how much of the time do we simply register the fast flowing types of energy in which we are immersed? We live perhaps more automatically than we realise. When we do think, what do we think about? If it does not conform to standard accepted patterns we are soon condemned as freaks, rebels and troublemakers. This the youth in our

schools discovered. They were condemned for thinking in-
dependently. They rebelled.

Surely it will repay us to take a little time at the end of
each day to review what that day has included by way of
thought. How much we have thought and what we have
thought about makes us what we are. "As a man thinketh
in his heart, so is he".

In ordinary parlance we consider anything which is
effective as practical. To the mind, getting results is only
conceivable in relation to what it knows. If the mind knows
nothing about soul values all ideas relating thereto are impractical. It is impossible to rationally consider practicality
unrelated to an objective. The human soul using the mind
has objectives superior to the objectives of the personality.
There are considerations and values in soul consciousness,
which are intensely practical for its own objectives, which
have no effectiveness for the more restricted materialistic
objectives of the personality. To the amazement of the expanding mental consciousness, the practicality of the soul
potencies demonstrating increasingly superior power has to
be admitted even while not yet understood. This liberates
personality emotional desire to gain soul consciousness.
Thus the personality becomes a spiritual aspirant. The
drive of the process of evolution itself will make every man
a spiritual aspirant someday, but any man can step forward
ahead of that slow evolutionary process if he so chooses.

Spiritual aspiration is an epic step in evolution in want-
ing spiritual values more than material values. It is a point
of victory for the human soul. It opens the door to a new
expanded consciousness. To help men to become spiritual
aspirants is direct cooperation with God's Plan for man.
The goal of material success is inherently separative and
competitive. The goal of spiritual aspiration is inherently
integrating and cooperative. The aspirant, whether he
knows it or not, has begun to seek soul contact and has
started to leave behind greed, injustice and cruelty. He is
no longer blocking the spiritual progress of mankind. He
has changed from a liability to an asset.

In the first stages of spiritual aspiration the individual is still motivated by the "more for me" goal but now there is a new transmuting factor which ultimately supersedes the separative competing desire drive because it is a vital characteristic of the goal of evolution itself. Once the aspiration is stabilised the man can delay for a time, but only for a time. Speaking symbolically, God must be very familiar with the prayer, "Dear God, make me a saint, but not too soon", and with the beginner in discipleship who prefers "a little discipleship as convenient".

We live in a dangerous era, between the old Piscean age and the new Aquarian age. Change is inevitable and quick. The lower mind seeks progress provided it does not upset accepted ideas, at least not much. The new age mind welcomes change and is daring. It knows that change in goals and in understanding life values is needed now or human suffering will increase and God's Plan be long delayed. To him the lukewarm is inadequate but he is no Piscean fanatic. Again, speaking symbolically, the great weapon of the devil is fear and also in getting individual, little-minded men to fight him. "Resist not evil but do good" is a profound spiritual concept. Many do not dare to stop resisting evil. The churches still seek to outdo the devil at his own game by condemning evil and using fear of punishment if you do not join in condemning sinners. The churchman controls the obedient followers by telling them what sin is and who are sinners. The church-controlled man dares not let go of this doctrine that the devil is very real and alive, that hell is real and that God, the Father of us all, sends people there. Therefore, the more intelligent humanity gets the more the church loses power. They fear a new, less childish, more reasonable religion. They dare not think new thoughts. This may sound drastic but Pope Paul and Billy Graham are in agreement today about hell and satan.

Entering the new age takes a bit of daring. The Christ needs fearless disciples. Courage is a spiritual asset. This is one of the fruits of strong faith. In the old days faith was belief in outer authority and did not require reasonableness. In the new age faith will be even more powerful in controlling life because it will transcend belief in outside authority and become reasonable, inner conviction. Then man will say truly, "I know whereof I have believed". The effect of spiritual values will become very practical indeed.

Soul Consciousness

After the present root race goal of mind control has been achieved, the next goal for human evolution will be the achievement of soul consciousness by the mass of men.

We are now increasingly valuing cooperation and good-will and the old Piscean age emphasis on being saved is giving way to the new age note of service to others and the common good. This is an essential characteristic of the new age of Aquarius.

Meanwhile some thousands out of the four billion human beings have already achieved the next great goal for all men and have some degree of soul consciousness. The top grade in this vanguard we call the Elder Brothers, the Masters of the Wisdom and, significantly enough, Lords of Compassion. Compassion is an aspect of love, and love is in fact the greatest thing in the world and is increasingly so recognised. These men are the members of the spiritual Hierarchy of the planet which is charged with the task of helping man to demonstrate God's Plan. This Hierarchy is a group of world executives and is as real as any board of directors of any modern multinational corporation and much more powerful. (The Hierarchy and its work is dealt with in the book *Running God's Plan*). Thousands who have a degree of soul consciousness know about this Hierarchy and aid in its work. These people we call "accepted disciples". The Christ, the head of the Hierarchy, needs the cooperation of many intelligent disciples.

We may wisely ponder on soul consciousness and accept it as our personal next step in evolution. Many of us have read diligently what has been said about the human soul but have pondered on it all too little. There is a tremendous amount of literature about the soul, for down the ages the fact of the soul has been taught. Most of this teaching is however more appropriate for a child stage of development than for the present time. But what all world religions have taught about the soul has built a foundation for soul knowledge and soul living and the fact of the human soul is no new idea.

Let us therefore take what we know about the characteristics and qualities of the soul and by focussing on it open ourselves to its influence. This is a practical way of expanding our consciousness and will make us more useful to our fellowmen sooner.

The personality even when highly evolved is self-conscious and separative. The soul is group conscious. The Piscean way of progress was by individual achievement. The Aquarian way is in group formation. When D.K. first spoke of group initiation many said yes, largely because they did not quite like to say no, but it meant little. So it is also about most new age teaching.

We have much to gain by pondering on group consciousness. Our first reaction is that it is a sacrifice of ourselves and our right to be. In fact it is the road to freedom. We gain the wisdom and the potency of the group and remain in control of our own lives. We understand the soul as a part of the one life and so find it at first difficult to understand how it is perfectly blended with all life, but that condition is no more impossible than our present ability to identify ourselves with a religion or an ideology or a social class. It is a matter of degree. We as individuals have a divine destiny and so also the human family as a whole has a divine destiny and these two destinies are in fact not antagonistic. The human family's destiny perfects the individual destiny. It does not destroy it. A right group focus and objective brings greater individual usefulness and, therefore, deeper poise and satisfaction. Insistence on going one's own way is not spiritual living. We as human beings need not be afraid to grasp larger concepts than we now fully understand. You can kill a man's body but you cannot kill a man. Let us therefore welcome group consciousness. It is an inevitable part of soul life and soul life is more free and more joyous than personality life.

What then of joy? Joyousness is a natural condition of soul consciousness arising from complete harmony in relationships. It does not depend on having things or on circumstances. It is as natural and constant to soul consciousness as breathing is to our physical life. It is the result of absence of conflict and is a soul condition because souls are never in conflict. It is not an emotion or a desire of the soul. It simply is. It seems curious that the soul can be joyous at the same time that the personality is sad but so it is in fact. It is not a wrong condition to be sad because of man's inhumanity to man. It is far better to be sad than to be hard-hearted. Being cast down and sad about what we want and because of our individual condition is degrading and weakening, but being saddened by present world suffering, cruelty and injustice is ennobling. It evidences the beginning of recognised group consciousness. Sadness is an aid to escape into joyousness. The Lords of Compassion are joyous because they are conscious free souls, but they are not happy about human suffering. Joy banishes fear and doubt and so brings strength to group spiritual endeavour. It is one of the most valuable attributes of soul consciousness.

Wisdom is a soul quality. Those who have complete soul consciousness, as we have said, are known as the Masters of the Wisdom. As the human mind evolves man knows more and more about a multitude of facts. One of these facts is that we are smothered in facts little understood and often wrongly used. Wisdom grows out of understanding rightly applied to life. It results from enlarged perspective and is a natural result of group consciousness and the application of knowledge to group good. Wisdom is therefore a soul characteristic and a natural soul asset. By achieving soul consciousness we achieve wisdom because the soul is more intelligent than the mind. The greater includes the lesser and as we grow spiritually we lose nothing gained by the mind.

As we ponder upon soul consciousness we discover that we know more about the human soul than perhaps we thought we knew. It therefore becomes more real to us. To realise that we can have soul consciousness is thrilling, and that we can hasten the process of acquiring it is exciting. There is nothing we can do which will make us more useful cooperators with the Christ than this focussing on gaining soul control. With more soul consciousness we can carry more Christ energy and use it more wisely.

Mystery Schools

Of late years esoteric students have become increasingly aware of the fact of the existence of the Mystery Schools of ancient days. It may be useful to gather more information about them, how they came into being, what type of training they offered. Are there schools today that provide similar training with similar goals? Will there be such schools in the new Aquarian age? The reasonable answer to these questions is Yes.

We know that there have been such schools for long ages in the past and as with past civilisations some knowledge exists but much is yet to be uncovered. The dates when they flourished are not known in most cases, nor are the names of their leaders, but that they were schools for discipleship, that they recognised the true divine man as the soul and that living as a soul was an attainable goal, were basic concepts presented by the Masters of the spiritual Hierarchy of the planet, in graded stages appropriate to the mental unfoldment of the humanity of their time.

There have been many such schools for discipleship in many lands, including China, India, Egypt, Persia, Chaldea, Yucatan and Palestine. The latest about which we know the most was in Greece located in Delphi and later moved to Crotona. It was presided over by Pythagoras.

That there are such schools in this century inspired from the same source is certain because discipleship is a definite stage of unfoldment of human evolutionary consciousness. That it will remain so in the new Aquarian age is not to be rationally doubted. That there is at least one school for discipleship now functioning which has the beginnings of new age characteristics is asserted. It does not advertise, makes no claims, charges no fees, is not secret, offers no separate personal powers, is not an escape from the discomforts of modern life, requires no oaths, promotes self-mastery and stresses mental freedom. Its leaders claim no high personal status nor powers. "By their fruits ye shall know them". It is not whispered by devotees to be a modern Mystery School. Its students do not go around promoting it.

Because of the resentments and persecutions by those in power whose continuing privileges were threatened by these ancient schools, there were strict rules of secrecy. At the end of the age it was foretold, and indeed it is so, that all things shall be revealed and "shouted from the housetops". The discomforts of opposition have not stopped, but extreme persecution largely has. Esoteric teaching is not secret in the modern world, just as secret diplomacy in national affairs has become not only a threat to democracy but not necessary for right national relations.

Advanced esoteric training is not useful for all, but is for those who qualify. The known fact that there is such teaching opens doors, now usefully opened as the race has become more intelligent. Modern esoteric teaching can no longer be hidden and need not be, but it suffers somewhat from publicised claims of quickly acquirable powers. The protection of the unready is not aided by mystery and secrecy today. That works automatically by the drop-out system, by the absence of glamorous claims and not by solemn oaths and rigid conformity.

The occult training schools of the Aquarian age will probably be non-secret, non-oath-taking, and will promote self-discipline voluntarily persisted in with maximum mental freedom. The ancient mystery schools will not be exactly duplicated. The new age schools will be markedly less mystical in teaching, and will in their higher stages give more advanced training than would have been useful in the old schools. This is now possible because mankind is growing up.

In the new age many more will qualify for training for discipleship and the total number of disciples in the human family will considerably increase. The new training will continue to require personal teaching and personal purity of life, including a higher degree of selflessness, and practical action as world servers will be undertaken at an early stage. More detail about God's Plan for man will be given and the training will be less for the progress of the pupil and more for the welfare of humanity. In the old days the discipline was long, arduous and strictly according to prescribed rules to which submission was required. We are now entering a new age of personal freedom and conformity will be voluntary, accepted because intuitively recognised as wise and reasonable by the inquiring mind.

In the old system the applicant generally enrolled for a prescribed time from which he could not thereafter honourably escape and definite freedoms of the personality had to be given up. Increasingly in the new age this will not be necessary or appropriate. Since humanity is growing up, it is not wise to treat a young man of twenty-one years as was necessary when he was twelve years old.

Discipleship training will be more consciously under the guidance of the Masters because greater fruitage will result that way, and it will be more possible, but there will inevitably be more and better assistant leaders useable by the Masters and they will be more characterised by humility. The fallacy of being more effective if their own powers and claimed status are recognised, will be superseded. They will be less and less able to attract followers by claiming that they have achieved this and that in their own consciousness, often showing pleasure when their devotees make that claim for them.

When an individual joins a legitimate occult training group for discipleship today he does not risk so much so blindly. He gambles his time and attention and effort at his own continuing pleasure. His goal is conscious obedience to his own soul, not to any leader or to the rightness of any set of rules prescribed by somebody else.

Although the esoteric schools of the future will be different from those of old in some respects, they will inevitably be essentially the same in method and goal. All the ancient Mystery Schools were linked with the Masters and all taught mind control by meditation. The new age schools will be the same in this and other respects. God's Plan for man remains essentially the same. Its presentation has changed as it unfolded in the past and will do so again.

Spiritual Tension

Spiritual evolutionary progress requires tension; likewise world adjustments for the good of humanity require tension. This tension becomes dangerous when ideologies fervently believed to be beneficial by masses of men are represented by governments that have great destructive power.

The trouble today is not world tension, but the misunderstanding of its significance. The goal is not to secure tranquility by easy-going tolerance or by condoning the continuance of the old age type of civilisation which crucifies the many for the benefit of the few. Human progress under the divine Plan and the law of evolution is inescapable. And by progress we recognise that we mean progress according to God's Plan for man rather than men's competition among themselves for what is conceived to be good for those who can get it.

The tensions that inevitably result from the present rapidly changing world progress are not the work of wicked men, though wicked men do exploit them. Tensions are neither good nor bad in themselves. When they become neurotic and menacing their removal cannot be brought about by the temporary expedient of using force. We must liquidate or render harmless the dangerous tensions by pressing forward to a world of peace with freedom, justice and decent living for all. This pressing forward in turn produces what we can rightly consider spiritual growth tension, which is very much to be welcomed. This recognition of the usefulness of spiritual tension, the welcoming of it, and the determination to take advantage of it, will tremendously augment the usefulness of the increasing thousands all over the world today who are giving their time and their energy and their money for human betterment.

Our function, as esotericists having knowledge of the Plan and of the Hierarchy, will continue within the esoteric field, but must be expanded from that field to those intelligent men and women of goodwill who have some world vision and interest in world affairs, and who are increasingly responding to the influence of the Christ as he approaches. Here is our field of growth. These people as a group in the body of humanity may well be recognised as lovers of humanity, just as we have developed, under the term patriots, people in various countries who are lovers of their nation. We recognise also that in reaching into this broader field we should not be propagandists, in the ordinarily accepted understanding of that term.

It would be abortive for us to try to understand these people whom we will increasingly reach, in terms of what they want, or what they will easily accept, or what will relieve them of their strain and confusion. The subtle desire to control and to lead and to dominate has historically proved a curse to organised religion as well as nations. This error must never victimise the new group of world servers. It is not our business to identify what we conceive to be acceptable truth, and then sell it to the intelligentsia. It most certainly is our proper function to bend every effort to ourselves better understand what these truths may be, and then to more rationally display them, being completely content to let those who hear and see react in their own good time in their own natural ways.

The need, as the esoteric group grows in the coming years, will be to increasingly identify and become aware of the work that the members of the new group of world servers are actually doing. We can identify world servers without listing them or seeking to influence them, but in practical ways aiding and cooperating in specific projects already underway. The true world server is already under a more potent and better directed influence than we can provide, and we should not be over-ambitious or over-credulous of our capacities. The esoteric group may yet discover itself being tested for spiritual humility.

New Age Hierarchical Work

The work of the Hierarchy produced the emergence historically of high disciples and inspired people in various fields of human expression. This included the emergence of a group of philosophers whose teachings conditioned the thoughts of men; the emergence of a group of musicians who produced a spiritual inlet into human consciousness by the majesty of their music; the emergence of a group of poets who expressed lofty thoughts in terms of rhythm which lifted human consciousness; and later the group of financiers who have understood money as an agency for the welfare of mankind.

In the midst of this practical and long-range effective action, the Hierarchy brought esoteric teaching to the West and created what we now recognise as a modern esoteric group, using H. P. Blavatsky as a spearhead disciple. As a result we have today many thousands of people who have a degree of esoteric knowledge which specifically includes and depends upon knowledge of the fact of God's Plan for the evolution of human consciousness and the existence of an organised hierarchical group who are custodians of that Plan often referred to as the Masters of the Wisdom. The teaching made available to esotericists under this hierarchical project has permeated more widely than is generally recognised and has coloured the thinking of many lovers of humanity. This has emerged because of the basic truth and reality of the teachings, in spite of the follies of separative, sectarian, dogmatic action in the esoteric field.

It is not unreasonable to recognise that the coordinating and interrelating of spiritual workers in all departments of hierarchical effort is one of the most significant new age projects of the Hierarchy itself. It was this potential usefulness that caused the Hierarchy in its council in 1925 to set in motion a closer cooperation between working disciples in the world than had ever been attempted before. The same action was evidenced within the Hierarchy itself in the relationship of various ashrams. For example, while the ashram of the Master Morya and the ashram of the Master Koot Humi have their continuing ashramic objectives and services, these two ashrams are today so closely and harmoniously related that for the senior disciples in those ashrams, they function almost as one.

In the same manner, gradually there is emerging in the modern world a realisation that those lovers of humanity who work for a better world for human beings to live in have an inner unified relationship which precipitates through increasingly in an outer harmonious and cooperative understanding. The growth of outer group usefulness, in response to this inner strengthening group unity, is a spiritual feature of the dawning new day.

This change of vision applies specifically to the life of the disciple. And those disciples who see this emerging trend and those aspirants to discipleship who seek to participate in spiritual world events, are increasingly subject to a new type of Aquarian cooperation which is an outer expression of an inner at-one-ment.

In the midst of this accelerating process what of the esotericists of the world? Is there a group destiny of expanded usefulness in the esoteric field? Nations as well as individuals grow by moments of crisis. What is done under tension produced by crisis determines the direction and the quality of our emergence into the new cycle. This applies also to the evolving consciousness of the esotericists of the world who can have a group effect on human thought and consciousness far beyond anything that has been achieved by this agency in the past. A thousand individuals all working for a chosen goal, voluntarily accepted by all, is a powerful instrument for human good if the goal is indeed good. But at best it is but the beginnings of that Aquarian group consciousness in action which lies at the heart of the spiritual growth of the future.

If the esotericists of the world simply ride along with the emerging new age tide there will be slow growth and little usefulness. The two inevitably go hand in hand as we face the future.

The more we know about group growth, the more wisely we can adjust our individual growth with the larger more important usefulness of the group future. Basically because of inner soul influence, we all want to do something about it and, in the doing, we will demonstrate in consciousness that we do not lose ourselves but have indeed found ourselves. In this process for the accepted working disciple, his personal problems and goals become incidental factors. He at last stands free. The spiritual quality of the lives of the serious esoteric students in the world can be combined and made useable in the new day. Its potency depends upon the spiritual quality of the lives of those who constitute that group.

There is a deepening awareness in the esoteric field of individual responsibility for an increasing new age usefulness in hierarchical work. The old age motive of individual personal progress on the path is being swallowed up by the larger recognition of the more joyous and free consciousness of participation in the expanding spiritual consciousness of humanity. This needs understanding and facing, for if we do not look forward to greater group usefulness we shall forfeit our group heritage. An understanding of group spiritual usefulness is a matter of gradually expanding individual consciousness. But it need not now be as slow a process as would have inevitably been the case before 1945.

One way of getting at this process is by coming to grips with the future usefulness of the esoteric group within the esoteric field with which we are associated. Another way of getting at it is to ponder upon and deepen our understanding of the immediate objectives of the Hierarchy in their work for humanity at the present time. Still another way is our closer approach in understanding and cooperation with what the new group of world servers is doing in the world today. And yet another way is the renewed pressing forward to effectiveness in those spiritual objectives already entrusted to the esoteric group with which we are identified. In all these ways there is need of persistent effort.

Christ's Own People

One of the most important things being done by the esoteric group in the world today is the proclaiming of the fact of the occult Hierarchy of the planet. This gives reason and purpose and assured success of the spiritual evolution of humanity. Without it we are adrift in the seething waters of emotional self-interest with the human mind enslaved to material values. The story of the Masters of the Wisdom is now coming to the intelligent public as a reasonable foundational concept. Along with this a startling new concept of the reality of the Christ as the head of the Hierarchy is emerging. The Christ is increasingly being understood as a great world executive whose vision and purpose includes all religions and all work for human salvage in all the seven major fields of human development. He is now thought of as a real man in actual existence, preparing now to reappear very shortly among men. The devotees of churchianity do not like this and the devotees of Christianity do not readily welcome the breaking down of their claimed exclusive possession of him. The knowledge of who the Christ really is and of what he really does grows apace. It is a priceless gift to the confused and struggling mass of men. For the spreading of this truth the esotericists in the western world are responsible. Much more needs doing about it.

A renewed sense of usefulness in the modern world is growing among all who have increasing awareness of esoteric realities. What the esoteric group in the world has to offer in the present era is long-range vision, deeper understanding of God's Plan for man, the illumining of the values inherent in spiritual realities, the critical necessity for establishing a practical foundation for right human relations, a recognition of the Christ as he really is and more active preparation for his outward reappearance among men.

When Christ was here before, some two thousand years ago, it is reported that the promise was made that he would return. This promise has been variously interpreted through the intervening years. It is significant that this promise voices the same proposition which is also found in the other leading religions of the world whose followers do not base their belief in this respect upon the same words uttered on the same occasion. Annie Besant, in the theosophical world, was one of the first to place this idea in some reasonable context in her notable lecture on Avatars. And in our own more recent time the Tibetan has given us most valuable teaching about Avatars and helped us in our appraisement of the Christ in that fundamental technique of hierarchical work furthering God's Plan for humanity.

The orthodox Christians thought the return was to be at the end of the world when the whole scheme of human life on this planet was brought to its close and the sheep would be sorted from the goats, some going to heaven and some to hell. Growing out of this have been various crusades and organised movements, such as the Seventh Day Adventists, led by those who have responded, often unknowingly, to the reality in this basic concept and the great truth which it hides.

Toward the close of any age such spiritual ideas have taken root in the human family, always becoming encrusted with human limitations and so distorted that they get to the point where they are more of a handicap than they are of a help. This is true of the idea of the reappearance of the Christ. A fervent belief in the reappearance of the Christ based upon the old age notions about it is definitely a handicap in any attempt that we now make to be of assistance to that reappearance. It does, however, give a basis of belief of some sort in the reappearance at some time.

Fortunately, a rather negative "wait and see" attitude

was not enough to block the reception of the new statement of the imminent return, and we were greatly helped by the fact that the statement was put forward in an extremely rational and reasonable way and not as an idealistic dictum. Increasingly here and there response became dynamic, and we now have something more than mere loyalty to teachings.

It is reasonable to think that it may be useful to have a special group in the world, just as there is now a special group in the Hierarchy, which will be an inner core of conscious disciples who will emerge—probably not in any organised way, but more as the new group of world servers itself emerges. As Christ's own people such a group would have in it disciples on all the rays, disciples anchored in various ashrams, and disciples karmically linked with the Christ in special ways.

There are, of course, in the Christian world a great many people who respond to what they understand to be the Christ note. It is really in fact much more the Christian church note about the Christ than actually the Christ's note, but through that channel they do get a real touch of Christ potency. Others in other religions respond to the same note but use a different name and get their contact via another channel, or perhaps we might better say via another thread in the same channel—a thread of light. Some also touch the same direct stream purely through their humanitarian work and their efforts to relieve suffering and starvation and misery all around them.

We are now beginning to understand a little better that many things are definitely a part of the planned work of the Hierarchy under the Christ's great leadership, and must inevitably be harmoniously related to his basic, fundamental note and purpose and the work that he is now preparing to do for humanity. Thus we come to recognise that all seven of the hierarchical departments of work are parts of one effort now related to and in harmony with the project of preparation for the reappearance of the Christ. This worldwide refocussing of effort and vision of many disciples in many fields makes it appropriate that we should give consideration to a group contribution to this end.

Such a group as it emerges must be balanced. It certainly cannot be very successful if the note is predominantly mystical and old age and devotional, and if the action taken is motivated mostly by blind allegiance to the Christ. Serving the Christ must be the result of serving humanity, thus *sharing his motive.*

Those who respond to the impact of this developing special stream of Christ potency will inevitably be tested, as all disciples in all fields are tested, for perseverance; for the purity of their motives; for their impersonality; for their breadth of view; and for their effectiveness in actual constructive operations. Their approach to their work must be rational and increasingly command respect from the intellectuals of the world.

Only those people who are really useable can come very close to this group of Christ's own people. Response to the idealism can be a little step, but it is far from enough to carry the individual into the group. The soul must be controlling the life of the disciple to a very considerable extent; and the rampant personality, fighting for the preservation of its supremacy in the life, insisting on its right to be itself and on the great value of its own concepts and ideas, has to be merged more completely in the life and quality of *this* group than in any other group functioning in the new age now being experimentally tried out among the sons of men.

The receipt in the personality life of increased spiritual potency always upsets things. That sometimes hurts and sometimes is difficult and sometimes leads to side-tracks, and almost inevitably lets in glamour to some extent. Many people who would love to be one of Christ's own group will be tremendously spiritually exalted by the idea that they have so consecrated themselves, and they will go through an unhappy stage where many of them will get little childlike reflections of the messianic complex. Some of them will say and do extravagant things which the more rational will look on at with a sickening feeling that it is hurting Christ's work. Others will be very sure that they are now at last in personal contact with the Christ, and this will mean that every idea that comes into their heads about preparation for the Christ will for them be inspired and almost sacred. Others will proceed to get direct messages and will be shocked and hurt that their best friends do not seem to be as affected by these messages as they are. All such will fall away, but their recognition of the note will bring them renewed opportunity at a later date.

So it will be true that as this group forms it will go through the same sort of troubles that other discipleship groups have to go through. Nevertheless this group will be receiving hierarchical impression and spiritual stimulant and increased vision according to their capacity. Such a group, when it really is underway, will be utilised to the very extremity of what is safe for the group. It is the group that will receive the main contact from these higher sources, and individuals will help in creating the group contacts. These contacts will come from the new ashram created in the Hierarchy for preparation for the reappearance and from other ashrams to which these disciples are linked. As this proceeds the group itself will become the recipient of the new potency, and the usefulness of the group, as a group, will become paramount to the usefulness of any individual member in the group. And yet this cannot be achieved unless individual members in the group themselves achieve usefulness, and this they cannot do unless they consciously blend with the hierarchical note so that they in fact synchronise to some appreciable degree with the Christ energy as it pours in.

Until such a group has been tested and is receiving this new age Christ energy somewhat effectively, there will be definite risks involved in attempting to use it. It is therefore obvious that this new group of Christ's own people is not going to spring up overnight and is not going to become a popular cry, and that those who are gravitating in that direction do so in stages of *progressive intensification of the leading of the Christ life in the deepest, truest sense.*

The Shamballa Force

The Shamballa force is a first ray energy expressing the power of the spiritual will. This sustains the second ray energy of love and aids in producing love action by its will-to-good. The first manifestation is the destroyer aspect, breaking the power of all forms and organisations which hinder God's Plan, including ideas and thought habits which are leftovers from the Piscean age. This is not a pleasant process and produces pain. If we did not cling to our old habits, pain would die out and it eventually will. Pain results from resistance to spiritual progress and is an agent for good. Pain is a human phenomenon in the solar system.

> "Let pain bring due reward of light and love.
> Let the soul control the outer form and life and all events and bring to light the love that underlies the happenings of the time".

The Hierarchy does not work to release us from pain but to help us to profit by it.

The destroyer aspect of the Shamballa force is now over. It has done its work and no part of humanity remains untouched. The next aspect based upon the will-to-good is is about to be released in full force. The results are sure. This will-to-good is much stronger than human greed. The human family is successfully responding to the new age forces and the aid of Shamballa will be abundant. The United Nations, which has been grievously hurt by competing nations using it for their own separate gain, will have new strength and great worldwide influence.

Our new teaching about Shamballa brings word that Shamballa is the home of planetary peace. Hierarchy is a force centre in the body of humanity which is always in action, balancing the conflicts between the pairs of opposites. The life of the Masters of the Wisdom in the Hierarchy is not a quiet meditative peace but constant intense effort to aid God's Plan for man.

Shamballa is a force centre in the body of the Lord of

the World, Sanat Kumara. The energy of Shamballa holds all the activities of Sanat Kumara in one unified expression of His life. It combines and relates and coordinates life at all levels and in all its varied manifestations. It stills the noise of competition and soothes the strain of struggle.

The Shamballa energy brings to fruition the fourth ray of harmony and the final adjustment of all pairs of opposites, not the destruction of either. The goal when attained by mankind will enable the Lord of the World to proclaim, "Now naught remains that is not beautiful". Here we have a key to what beauty really is; transcending beauty of form is beauty in life quality. We know more about the other six ray qualities than we do about the fourth ray. When we become more conscious of Shamballa we shall know more about the fourth ray and respond to its influence more intelligently.

Motive controls the action in the life of all disciples co-operating with Hierarchy. Pure reason controls the action in Shamballa and pure reason requires pure motive. Therefore, Shamballa recruits come by way of Hierarchy and as a result of hierarchical training in service. Shamballa and Hierarchy are conscious cooperating parts of one planetary purpose. As humanity learns more about Shamballa we shall also become conscious cooperators with Sanat Kumara.

Both functions require a degree of personality-soul infusion which is evidenced in the way we choose to live, what we want most in life and our use of our minds. We get that way by our own persistent effort, but with lots of help. Once we have made the soul link and established a soul life rhythm, we progress best by selflessness, harmlessness and right speech, the three chief characteristics of the new group of world servers. To have a soul-infused personality requires an aligned, coordinated, concentrated personality motivated by love and controlled by *purpose*. So also is the life control of disciples in Shamballa.

We have been informed that prior to 1925 the human kingdom received the impact of Shamballa force only after it was stepped down in potency by passage through the Hierarchy. At that time a spiritual experiment was tried by Sanat Kumara to see how much humanity could take of direct Shamballa energy. The experiment was encouraging but the disrupting effects were great. Direct impact was tried in 1975 and again will be in the year 2000. It seems that these direct impacts take place in connection with the hierarchical conclaves when the whole Hierarchy is focussed on humanity and we have the maximum benefit of hierarchical attention and protection.

In 1975 the human family had the benefit of years of sustained action by Hierarchy to impregnate humanity with the quality of goodwill which is the expression of the will-to-good of Shamballa. This means that we can safely take more direct Shamballa force. We have now the force centre of the new group of world servers whose senior members can act as a consciously cooperating group. Also we now have the United Nations successfully anchored in the body of humanity, actively functioning, exoterically, and used by the Christ and the great interplanetary entity, the Spirit of Peace, both of whom now work through the General Assembly.

It is also of deep long-range significance that the Hierarchy is more closely related to Shamballa than ever before and this without doubt will be a prime characteristic of the new Aquarian age. The old Piscean age religion was focussed on individual salvation pictured by churchianity as escape from hell. The new Aquarian age religion will focus on group action for the benefit of all men. This will be aided by new age Shamballa force for this is the energy "which brings about synthesis and which holds all things within the circle of divine love".

The Avatar of Synthesis

The conquest of outer space by man has spiritual significance in preparing us to welcome human participation in solar evolution. That such participation will even be possible seems fantastic but the goal of human evolution on this tiny spaceship Earth includes that function. After all, is it so fantastic that the four billion human units now in incarnation, plus the untold millions not just now using physical vehicles, but very much alive, may have some part in the solar life of God. Let us pause and ponder again the concept that in due course we shall cooperate with Sanat Kumara and his purposes as we now seek to cooperate with the plans of the Christ.

One of the features of esoteric training consists in forcing the mind to reach out and attempt to grasp the significance of abstract truths. It is a valuable exercise, building in, as it does, new substance in the mental vehicle which is later a bridge between the concrete mind and spiritual perception coming from the soul. It is a practical occult step toward intuitive perception.

Other valuable aids in unfoldment for the spiritual aspirant are contemplation of aspects of esoteric teachings about the plans and purposes of Sanat Kumara, the goals and projects involved in the further evolution of the Masters of the Wisdom, and glimpses of the relation of our planetary objectives to activity in the solar system of which it is a part.

Such contemplation heightens the vibration of the mental body so that the personality can receive valid impressions from the soul. It hastens the day when the soul can take effective control of the life in the three worlds. Among these teachings for our pondering we now have available information about such extraplanetary entities as the Avatar of Synthesis. There is considerable information about this Avatar, particularly in Volume V of *A Treatise on the Seven Rays*.

It is interesting to note that increasing numbers of students have been contemplating the work of the Avatar of Synthesis. This has already produced a matrix of mental substance in the group mental body from which we can all benefit. This is true because of the automatic but generally unrecognised mental telepathic interplay which is increasingly available to us all, although very seldom precipitating all the way through to the physical brain cells. This is illustrated by the experience of many of us who find that in the presence of a keen, clear, powerful mind in another person we ourselves can think more clearly and to greater purpose. This also happens when we ponder spiritual writings.

Our first introduction to the fact of the assistance brought to our planetary process by the Avatar of Synthesis and made available to the new age work of the Christ is presented in the book *The Reappearance of the Christ*. His cooperation with the Christ dates from June 1945. By seeking to understand the significance of this very powerful aid from a new source (related directly to the immediate objective of Sanat Kumara) we can be greatly helped in our understanding of the relationship of the work of the Christ and the Hierarchy, not only to ourselves and to the solving of the problems of humanity, but also to the problems peculiar to the Hierarchy in its own evolution, to relationships between much more advanced Beings beyond the Hierarchy, and to the planetary goals with respect to solar destiny.

In this condition of mental stimulant, we find ourselves in a condition that we might call "mental sleeplessness". But in this type of contemplation we experience no sense of discouragement or futility because it carries with it a new spiritually sustaining potency. This is particularly true as we search into the significances of the work of the Avatar of Synthesis, grasping at such fragments of knowledge about it as are available.

The Avatar of Synthesis does not work with individuals —with the exception of the Christ himself—and his influence does not extend below the mental plane. Nevertheless, the influence reaches humanity because the focussed attention of the Avatar of Synthesis affects the mental body of the whole human family. In the stumbling efforts of the would-be server of his fellowmen, it becomes easier to maintain the steady focus needed.

One of the results has been stated to be a stimulation of

the will-to-do. And it is significant that it is not simply a heightened vibration, but a definite quality especially useable by men and women of goodwill. The weakest link at the present time in the goal of conscious relationship of humanity to the Hierarchy is the inertia of the men and women of goodwill. This greatly slows down our solving of the problems of humanity. The increased will-to-do has significant usefulness here. When this condition can be lifted much swifter progress will result and the influence on the mental bodies of the men and women of goodwill, resulting from the focussed attention of the Avatar of Synthesis, is destined to bear rich fruitage indeed.

The same advantage accrues to the focal points in the human family which we call nations. National consciousness is directly affected by the work that the Avatar of Synthesis is doing through the channel of the General Assembly of the United Nations. This increases a spontaneous urge towards unity which is a stabilising influence and produces a hastening of achievement of right national relationships as a step towards right human relationships.

The new conditions confronting the Christ as he seeks to fit himself for successful action in the Aquarian age are more stupendous than we have yet been able to realise. They include many factors which have as yet little direct application to the present day problems of humanity as we seek to deal with them in practical terms. The cooperation of the Avatar of Synthesis brings supporting strength and aids the new deepening vision of the Christ himself. We have been told that, owing to the stupendous task confronting the Christ, the Avatar of Synthesis will fortify him and "keep His eye upon him, His hand beneath him, and His heart in unison with his".

As we contemplate such a possibility, we are helped to more definitely appreciate the fact that the Christ is not some mysterious, distant, mystical entity, but that he is a practical, active, spiritual executive who has taken on the load of special usefulness to humanity in the Aquarian age, in addition to his own spiritual evolutionary necessities. The more real the Christ becomes to us in rational, understandable terms, the more the energies which he is pouring into humanity can find anchorage in our own consciousness. There is a new deepening understanding of who and what the Christ is, rapidly emerging in the minds of esoteric students. This is an important factor in changing human consciousness sufficiently so that his reappearance can be hastened.

Transmuting Materiality

It might well be said that we have trouble enough in the physical plane problems now confronting humanity without burdening ourselves with what might somewhat inaptly be called the problems of the Hierarchy with regard to their own progress into future usefulness. It is to be remembered, however, that the foundation on which all esotericism has always rested is the fact of the existence of the spiritual Hierarchy of the planet. All the ancient Mystery Schools were founded thereon. It is significant that those seeking to implement our efforts have seen fit to greatly increase our knowledge of the Hierarchy, its purpose and its function and its destiny, particularly during the last fifty years.

We sometimes forget that the imparting of new and advanced teaching about spiritual realities requires sustained, focussed attention on the part of some Master and the expenditure of considerable energy. When the Master works in the three lower worlds he becomes subject to the laws governing those planes, although less so than are we. It has been no light task to create a sufficiently integrated esoteric group in the world so that this new teaching could find anchorage and a modicum of intelligent response.

As this process goes on we come closer in consciousness to the Hierarchy than otherwise would be possible because the whole field of spiritual reality becomes more rational and its effects are recognised as more practical. This helps us transcend the limitations of the purely mystical approach and is an aid in hastening the day when the rapidly developing mental body of humanity will reorient itself in the light. Then we shall have achieved on the physical plane not escape from materiality but a transmutation of its main characteristic as it now functions, which is selfishness, leading to separative ruthless grasping.

We have been like children in our blind allegiance to materiality. And for all practical purposes there are great masses of men today who really live for the fulfillment of their desires based upon three achievements: to get more money, to buy more things, to have more fun.

This slavery of humanity to materiality has now climaxed and the thoughtform built by the minds of men is now a gigantic, powerful dweller on the threshold. Before the human mind could be reoriented, a surgical operation on the mental plane had to take place. And it was the direct application to humanity from Shamballa of the destroyer aspect of the first ray which did the work. It is said that this potency split this gigantic human thoughform on the mental plane. This was in fact a great spiritual event preceding the resulting present worldwide struggle in which we now suffer but from which we are already beginning to emerge.

This splitting of the enslaving thoughtform of materiality which we had built let in the light with the result that the Hierarchy will now be more effective in aiding us than was heretofore possible. It goes to the very heart of the significance of the first stanza of the Great Invocation because now light can "stream forth into the minds of men" in abundant effectiveness.

We have been told that the spiritual Hierarchy of the planet will in the days to come be a body of men who will be much superior to the personnel in the Hierarchy in ages gone by. This is the result of the fact of the process of growth which goes on at all levels and at all stages of consciousness, including the Christ himself.

In attempting to speak of these things and in letting our minds play upon them we are indeed like children, knowing little but daring much. We have to learn to speak definitely about such matters without being dogmatic.

There are other significant events occurring in the reorganisation of the Hierarchy in preparation for the reappearance of the Christ about which we have some knowledge. Ultimately there will be forty-nine ashrams in the Hierarchy and the process of perfecting them is well underway. This involves opportunity for many high-grade accepted disciples who heretofore have stayed much longer on the periphery of the Hierarchy before participating in direct ashramic action. The newly accepted disciple causes more difficulty in the Hierarchy as to its internal adjustments than any other one factor.

Two things have been accomplished in the Hierarchy of recent times: one, the closer welding of the work of the seven major ashrams and the other, the focussing of the main hierarchical effort on the three departments of government, religion and education.

When we contemplate the energies which the Christ now wields, recognising their complexity and the necessity of integrating and blending them, we get an added appreciation of one of the most important functions of the Christ today. He is, of course, still handling the tremendous potency of the Piscean era, out of which we are passing but which still powerfully affects the majority of human beings on this planet. To ignore it would be the height of folly. This has to be increasingly blended with and adjusted to all the new potencies. In addition, the resulting effects in human consciousness of what has been the dominating sixth ray are by no means over, particularly in the United States. Here again we have the task of skillful adjustment and modification.

How far it is wise and how much is possible to produce constructive progress in bringing in the new age which inevitably arouses human fear and rebellion, is one of the big problems the Hierarchy and the Christ in their executive capacities have confronting them. Humanity is being given today every last bit of new age influence that it can possibly constructively absorb.

The above very sketchy and inadequate thoughts give us just a glimpse of the stupendous effort required and the long-range importance of the position that the Christ has assumed as head of the Hierarchy for the coming age. We give these energies names but we do not really yet have the capacity to understand them. It is, however, very useful and an aid in the preparation for the reappearance of the Christ to have a group of esotericists in the world who know more about what is required of the Christ in the new age than we have ever known before.

Solar Evolution

There was a time when we had no knowledge of the existence of the solar system. The idea of a solar system was utterly unknown. The discovery of that idea was one of the greatest events in all human history. The fact that a human mind can grasp it proclaims that mankind has potential solar importance. The evolution of human consciousness is a part of a solar process which it is not responsible to consider as confined to one small planet.

What do we know about our solar system at the beginning of the last quarter of the twentieth century? All that we now know are only fragments of what we shall know, are incomplete and subject to great change as human consciousness continues to expand, and it is well to keep this in mind. How large is a universe is now a question about which we can glimpse an answer. We have identified objects which we call quasars, which are so far distant that it takes their light billions of years to reach this Earth, and we now estimate that our universe is fourteen billion years old.

There are scientific indications that there are millions of solar systems and we are quite safe in accepting this as fact. This involves the recognition that our solar system is not of great importance in the cosmic manifestation. It is, however, of greater importance to us than we have heretofore known. We are now sending our spacecraft beyond our solar system with scientific recording instruments and this may well be the greatest human achievement we have ever made. It will inevitably ultimately expand our under-

standing of what life is. As we identify our solar systems
we can intelligently relate our own system to them. That
there is a plan and a purpose behind the manifestation of
our solar system is not an unreasonable concept.

So also there is a plan and purpose and an originating
cause behind the existence of our planet Earth with its five
kingdoms, and also of the individual units in those kingdoms. You and I have a place in the vast scheme of all
that is and it is this fact that gives value and dignity to
our existence.

The late president of the United States, John F. Ken-
nedy, was a solar pioneer. He launched the U. S. government into space exploration. We now have evidence that
our solar system and other solar systems are expanding in
space and that some solar systems are contracting. This
may indicate that human consciousness will continue to
expand and that the marvel and the glory of man has only
just begun. All this increasing knowledge about life itself
and of divine plan and purpose is paralleled by knowledge
of the substance out of which our solar system is built and,
therefore, of planets and of human beings.

All life manifests in units we call entities and we recognise man himself as a spiritual entity. The understanding
our new knowledge brings us about the solar system may
reasonably include the idea of a solar Logos. In Masonry,
He is called the Grand Architect of the Universe and also
the Great Geometrician, and Masonry is rightly regarded as
a spiritual quest, which is the purpose of humanity itself.

Humanity can understand our solar system better in
terms of a solar Logos than in terms of abstract energy. We
can understand that a solar Logos has a plan and a purpose
and that we have a part in it. So also, every planet in our
solar system can be comprehended as a spiritual entity
which we call a planetary Logos. The destiny of our planetary Logos is part of the destiny of our solar Logos and
can be rightly related to that larger destiny, or our solar
system plan and purpose will be a failure. In like manner,
the plan and purpose of the human kingdom on this Earth

must be rightly related to the destiny of our planetary Logos or His purpose fails and this destiny, we are taught, we must ourselves achieve. Thus science is making philosophers of us all and hastening the emergence of God's Plan.

We stand in awe of the wonder of God's Plan for man as revealed to us by scientific research in the final quarter of the twentieth century. What shall be revealed in the last quarter may well be far beyond our wildest dreams.

Science now tells us that there are millions of solar systems and that our solar system revolves around a greater force centre in the Milky Way. We call the controlling energy God, and Einstein said he could not conceive of creation without an intelligent God. Many leading scientists agree and it is not unintelligent to believe in God.

Scientific knowledge never stops growing. We used to be told that our sun had nine planets revolving around it, then a tenth was discovered, and now the location of an eleventh is identified and its size determined. Will there be a twelfth known to us in due time? Does it now exist? If so, does it affect our Earth, and therefore us, in some subtle way?

The evolution of the human mind is as great a marvel as any we know about. Its coming revelations are unlimited. Senator Fulbright (of the U.S.A.) called upon us to think the unthinkable and we are forced by science to do so. What was unthinkable a few years ago we now think about. Why put a limit on what we will be thinking about in the year 2000? Freedom of thought is the most powerful building tool man has. Dictators say only I—never you— can use it. There are disguised would-be dictators in the United States today. The Watergate scandal helped us save our freedom but the fight is not yet won.

The wise teacher known to many as Djwhal Khul, is a philosophical solar scientist. He is said to know more in that field than most other members of the Hierarchy. It is reasonable to think that when the Christ reappears and walks our streets again, he will work as a scientist as well as in other ways. Would it not be foolish to limit himself to religion? Surely he will not come to save the Christian religion. He will come to help us save ourselves. Surely he will not be a dictator. He will need intelligent cooperators, not just followers. For this we can begin to prepare. Let us ponder on this.

What will he most probably do? He will work as scientists work but without any self-imposed limitations. He will work with the tremendous power of goodwill which is love in action. This power is already flooding humanity and will increase. He will use the power of "the centre where the will of God is known", increasing the will-to-good among men. He will open wide the door to Shamballa as the door to Hierarchy is now open. We will know more about God's Plan for man than ever before and much sooner because he comes. Pondering these things is indeed thinking yesterday's unthinkables and is a soul-satisfying, daring adventure. Preparing for the reappearance of the Christ is a joyous way to live.

Science

Let us take a quick look at what science has already given us, remembering as St. Paul put it, "Now we see as through a glass darkly". With increasing power we need increasing humility lest in our blind greed we destroy ourselves.

We can create a human baby in a glass retort in a laboratory and are on the brink of controlling the gender of all natural born babies. What will the human family be like by the end of this century? Will that power be wisely used? Shall we just drift along or shall we think about it now?

We are beginning to control the weather on a planetary scale. We have made rain artificially, locally, for military purposes in war time. June 15, 1974, scientists from seventy nations began a 100-day weather research in the South Atlantic Ocean from outer space to ocean floor covering a 20-million square mile area. About forty ships and over a dozen heavily instrumented aircraft and earth orbiting satellites and ground stations took part. Scientists describe the area as "the boiler of the giant heat engine that runs our atmosphere". About four thousand scientists, technicians, observers and ship and aircraft crews participated. Russia financed one-third of the ships. When man controls the weather, what nation or group of nations will determine what weather and where? International cooperation for the greatest good for all men has become a must.

Weather control has long-range as well as short-range effects. If we reduce the moisture content of Earth's atmosphere over a long period of time and we do not put it back, we precipitate the death of humanity itself. Those planets that have no water have no human life. Slowly we learn that nature's resources on Earth are exhaustible. As we control nature we must control ourselves lest we die. Lack of knowledge, and greed, can bring race suicide. If our increasing knowledge continues and we use it wisely, greed-controlled human life on Earth will disappear. This is a hard fact. It does not affect the cost of tomorrow's breakfast but is far more important.

Science can now measure the temperature of the Earth. Our planet is getting cooler and has been since 1940. The difference between a global ice age and present conditions is only a matter of a few degrees in global temperature. When will this natural cooling process stop and are we helpless about it? Science says no we are not and even predicts that man's economic activity, if uncontrolled, could overheat the Earth.

Humanity, especially the people of the underprivileged nations, will need and use more energy, not less, as the years slip by. Atomic power can give us more than we need for everybody. The process of releasing energy includes releasing heat into Earth's atmosphere. This, if unrestricted, raises the temperature of the planet. This may sound fantastic but science says it is a real danger. Harnessing solar heat is a way out. Increasing release of carbon dioxide into the air is also a danger. By the year 2000 this release will have increased by up to 20 percent and will be a danger. Fewer cars going slower with less powerful engines will cut the main cause of this increase. We would be healthier if we walked more and our speed craze gains us no real values.

Volcanic action discharges vast quantities of dust into the air and periods of great volcanic action are followed by cold waves. Modern man produces a total of even more dust and science now measures this dust air content which cuts off the heat Earth gets from the sun. Science has proved that air pollution is a real danger to human life. Shall we just drift along until the planet becomes uninhabitable? Man heedlessly makes the planet hotter and also at the same time, colder. We can, therefore, control global temperature. Should we not so live that we maintain a constructive balance? Science says we can.

Man's conquest of space is a scientific achievement. We now know that other planets affect our planet and, therefore, the human kingdom and each one of us. Astronomers now say it is probable that life analogous to human life exists on other planets. We now put scientific instruments on far distant planets that give us data unknown a few years ago. Scientists now propose a coordinated international research program avoiding duplications and saving time and money, so getting more knowledge faster and at less cost. This is real international cooperation.

In August 1973, we got our first look at the surface of Venus which is mainly a landscape of shallow craters some 100 miles wide and 1,000 feet deep. Clouds around Venus are 13 miles thick but we have a map of parts of the surface. Venus has a high pressure atmosphere, no water, and only mild winds.

A grand tour by spacecraft to the most far-distant planets, including Jupiter and Pluto, is planned for about 1978 and on April 8, 1973, man first saw the edge of the universe. Now our spaceships have passed beyond that area limit.

Mariner 10 blasted off October 30, 1973, for Mercury via Venus. It was equipped to send back some 8,000 television pictures of both planets. The temperature of Mercury is about 650 degrees.

Jupiter is the largest planet in our solar system and is half a billion miles further from the sun than the Earth. Jupiter has twelve satellites or moons and its aura extends out over four million miles. It spins so fast that it has only a ten-hour day. Jupiter's radiation belts and surrounding magnetic field are very large and Mariner 10 sent back new data on them. The Mariner 10's closest approach to Jupiter's surface was 81,000 miles on December 3, 1973. It takes 11.86 years for Jupiter to go once around the sun.

In addition to planets there are nebulas in space which science identifies and studies. One of the oldest is the Gum Nebula, a vast cloud of gas and dust particles 128 light-years away from our Milky Way. A light year is six trillion miles. The temperature of the Gum Nebula gas cloud is 90,000 degrees, compared to 10,000 degrees for our sun.

The universe is expanding. Will it ever start contracting? Some scientists say yes. Others say no, holding the theory that it will continue to expand until it explodes. Others say it is infinite in time and space. There are objects in space called quasars over twice as far away as any other identified objects. They radiate brilliant light and radio waves. They have been thought to live forever and taken as evidence that our universe will live forever.

We could go on piling up data about what exists outside our planet. Until recent years it had been considered useless knowledge for the individual man. We are increasingly realising that this is not so. Knowledge about our solar system and everything in it expands our consciousness and that is a main goal of the evolution of the human kingdom itself. As man evolves, mind power increases and we demand that our concepts about right life values must be reasonable. If a young man in his twenties does not have his own ideas as to what is right and good for him and for others around, he is not much of a man. The modern youth movement is made up of young people who want to be men. If we older people do not meet that demand we are indeed foolish. Increasing solar knowledge is a major factor in the evolution of mankind. Mind power grows by use. When we contemplate the solar system we stretch the mind, which makes it grow faster and more wisely than its self-centred use to make money. The scientific conquest of space is of tremendous value to us all.

We have been talking about universes of material substance. What of universes composed only of mental substance? Is there such a thing as mental substance? The ancient secret Mystery Schools said yes. We are learning more and more about solar life and know that human life on Earth is only one kind of life or should we say one aspect of the life of God in our particular solar system.

And what of human consciousness which seems to be expanding through the ages? Is there an ultimate limit to that? Our conquest of space is bringing a tremendous expansion of human consciousness to which we do not need to postulate any end.

Science now considers that galaxies, or great star systems, are flying apart and therefore expanding. It is suggested that our universe originated in an enormous explosion of matter some fourteen billion years ago. That theory is perhaps better than no theory. The farthest quasar yet identified is reported in both Britain and America and appears to be moving away from our Milky Way. There is little doubt now that such cosmic objects exist. Our universe seems to be expanding at a uniform rate, that is to say, still exploding. Is it like a stone thrown into the air still moving out, but inevitably due to stop and begin to move back? Or will it ultimately explode and disintegrate thus ending universal life? This proclaims the wonder of that marvelous human thing we call consciousness. It may be that what is expanding is human consciousness, not the material universe.

One of the greatest breakthroughs since the atomic energy success is almost upon us in photographing the etheric aura of plants, animals and man. This attacks the problem in terms of light and for many years scientific dictum has included the statement that every known atom

when appropriately stimulated gives off its own characteristic light.

The latest developments in aura photography are a Russian achievement, supported by the government. This is
now being supplemented in the United States without government funds and hindered by leftover old age dogmatism.
It is known as Kirlian photography, from the name of the
Russian scientist who developed a device which produces
pictures of etheric substance. In the United States, leaders
in this field include Thelma Ross and Kendall Johnson.
The editor of *The Osteopathic Physician* magazine, D. J.
Chapman, has stated that many past civilisations have held
the tradition of an invisible energy pervading the universe.
The Egyptians called it *Ka*, the Hindus, *Prana*, the Chi-
nese, *Chi*, the Hawaiians, *Mana*. It was used in healing.
This energy substance interpenetrates all physical solids,
liquids and gases just as gases interpenetrate liquids and
solids. It then emerges that the human physical body is
composed of all four, and we have an energy body that can
be photographed.

The great new word of science is *energy*. We live in a
sea of energies in constant motion. This motion we speak
of as vibration and its potency increases with speed.

An atom is an energy unit. So also is a man. Atomic energy units are held together by a more potent energy, magnetic in quality, and capable of control by man. When this
binding energy is made inoperative the energies in the atom
fly apart and tremendous power is released which was before balanced, relatively inert, and in that condition a
stable factor in nature.

The energy maintaining an atom as a unit is far greater
than all the energies inside the atom. So also is the energy
of the human soul far greater than all the energies of the
mind, the emotions and the physical atoms of the personality. A personality is a unit of energy, coordinated, synchronised and held together by a superior energy unit, the
human soul. "Let the soul control the outer form and life
and all events and bring to light the love that underlies the

happenings of the time". This is the immediate goal of the esoteric student practicing an occult type of meditation and exemplifying selflessness in service.

To successfully operate a computer it is necessary to know about computers. So also to successfully operate our physical, emotional and mental bodies we need to know more about them. Therefore the esoteric student does not seek to escape from them in consciousness but to control them for use in God's Plan. This control by the true self might be rather inadequately expressed as the problem of the soul, and when at long last the personality begins to cooperate the whole process is tremendously hastened.

In the long process of evolving our physical bodies we have achieved the use of five senses bringing us physical plane consciousness. We have been in error in limiting our consciousness to these five senses and what they can control because there are aspects of life in a physical body which they do not register. The new day of science is with us because of the scientific recognition of realities not known to the five senses as thus far developed in man. These senses are still evolving and our physical brains also are evolving. To all this we are in the process of adding emotional senses which will give us emotional stability and which the physical brain can register. There is an emotional world which in many ways is more potent than the physical world and emotional energy is more powerful than physical energy. Physical energy cannot control emotional energy but mental energy can. Soul energy can control all three. Therefore let us increase the soul control of our lives.

Our planet has an etheric body which is in constant motion and which consists of minute streams of energy carrying the potency of the life of physical plane substance. Of late years science has been able to record, study and work with this planetary substance. This breakthrough is a major advance in evolutionary consciousness on this planet and, when scientifically applied to individual man, will complete the human mastery of the entire seven subplanes of our physical plane.

Our planet also has an emotional body consisting of seven subplanes of that type of solar substance which is the natural field of expression of our emotional life. The four most subtle of these subplanes correspond to the etheric body of the physical plane, are in constant motion and carry the potency of that type of solar energy we identify as emotion. This is duplicated in mental substance also. The emotional level etheric substance vibrates at a much higher speed than physical plane substance and the mental etheric still faster.

When in incarnation the soul has three bodies built of the substance of these three planes. When the energies of all three bodies, constituting a personality, are harmoniously synchronised with soul energy we achieve perfection in the three lower worlds. This includes perfect health, which the Masters of the Wisdom have.

Esoteric teaching tells us that the seven planes of our solar system constitute the seven subplanes of the cosmic physical plane, and each solar plane has seven subplanes. A cosmic Logos functioning on seven cosmic planes uses 343 grades of substance which exist as a unit in a veritable sea of cosmic energies.

Our at present materially limited minds now deal with three of these 343, plus the four physical ethers treated as one, or about one percent. This is for us mere theory, but in any event so-called exact science is a myth. We are, for example, becoming less sure that there is any such thing as a straight line. The danger to our consciousness in limiting human knowledge by science lies in the fact that science itself is so very limited. The non-scientific mind, as thus far evolved, fears the unknown and is relieved to think that it can be ignored. To suggest that we are wrong to believe in anything we cannot prove is a childish limitation not shared by the modern scientist.

THE SACRED WORD*

There has been a modern revival of the use of the sound OM, particularly in group meditation, and we may note that the word "Amen" is a corruption of that sound used basically as a materialistic affirmation or, at best, as a mere religious formalism with no knowledge of its spiritual significance.

The AUM which has sounded through long ages in the human family will die out as the involutionary process of divine manifestation is completed. It has brought the soul-spirit aspect down onto the physical plane, there to obtain mastery by experience. It has been likened to a strong wind that holds a man against a wall, making his own efforts difficult. Its sound vivifies material form and increases the hold of matter over the soul. It has built the prison of the five senses in which man has lived until now, but from which science is enabling us to escape. The AUM is the sound of enchantment, producing maya, glamour and illusion, a word of our childhood days. Here we may recall that childhood is necessary to produce manhood and that humanity has now come of age.

The body of the solar system in the substance of the third etheric plane is now built and nothing can stop the process of evolution in our solar system. The solar Logos is then said to be coordinated. The solar body is now complete but not yet perfected, but "consciousness thrills through every atom in the system". The lesser builders (devas) are literally "a sea of fire" on which the great breath, or AUM, takes effect.

There is also a seven syllable Word which has a letter for each of the seven Heavenly Men. Sanat Kumara has been called "the experimenting Divine Physicist". Hu-

---

* Reprinted from the May/June 1977 issue of *The Beacon* magazine.

manity is a divine experiment now proving successful. The manifestation of our solar Logos produces a total of twenty-one sounds and the right use of sound is a major goal of humanity. We have temporarily smothered ourselves with noise and sound discords. Jazz is a climaxing destructive use of sound.

Certain words or mantric sounds, uttered by a great Life, can drive the life in humanity to the fulfillment of constructive purpose. They are uttered by a solar Logos, a Heavenly Man, a Monad and an Ego in varying degrees.

There are many sacred words. We are dealing here with two, *i.e.,* AUM and OM. The latter is not an expression of the former and the effects produced are different. For humanity at its present stage of evolution the OM is needed. Rightly sounded it releases the soul from glamour. It is a sound of liberation from the matter aspect of divine manifestation which is the immediate goal of humanity. The AUM anchors the soul-spirit aspect on the physical plane. It vivifies form and intensifies the hold of matter on the soul.

The sound of the AUM moulds substance and creates forms. It also is as the sound of a raging fire burning up hindering, worn-out forms on all three personality levels. We still need to build forms for self-expression. And the world server can use the AUM to burn up all hindrances.

The AUM is the same signature in all languages. It is the sound produced by the first creative out-breathing of our solar Logos. Then came the OM. It is the most creative sound there is. The OM is a controlled withdrawal sound in the process of conscious control of form in man's return to God with the banner of victory in his hands.

D.K. suggests that we ponder on the distinction between the breath and the sound. The breath is related to time and the sound to space. Ultimately in this solar system both are transcended.

The disciple has learned the value of tension and does not seek to escape from that type of spiritual tension which is an expression of the human soul. The OM strengthens that tension. Personality tensions are a different matter and are overcome more by transcending, using soul tension, than by repression. Mankind will eventually achieve liberation from the three worlds at a point of spiritual tension, then standing at last as a truly free soul.

The most potent way to sound the sacred word is inaudibly within the head. When sounded audibly in group meditation, it should be quiet, not loud, and with a musical quality. This note emerges automatically in a group well trained in group meditation wherein the separated personal consciousness is merged into the group purpose chosen for the occasion. The thought held is that the *group* is sounding the word. The individual acts consciously as a part of the group.

The sound of the OM within the head is subtle and hard to describe. It has been called the soundless sound of the OM. It is not the sound of the consecrated personality but the sound of the soul. In the early stages of meditation and only as a beginning the aspirant sounds the OM audibly, recognising it as not the true perfected use of the OM. The OM when sounded with that intent becomes the disturber of the atoms of the mental, emotional, physical bodies, shaking out undesirable substance and building in new and more adequate material under the second Ray law of attraction. This actually takes place and is of practical value. For the best effects of the OM on the physical plane, idle speech should be abandoned. Indeed silence is golden and a spiritual asset. But right speech is also a spiritual asset and necessary in service. Before speaking think—is a wise rule.

To be most effective the person sounding the OM silently in the head should hold the significance of the word firmly in his consciousness. To know what one is doing and why always gives potency in action.

OM is the *sound of life*: it represents the great, rhythmic heartbeat of the Logos. It is the out-breathed life of God; it carries the energy and vitality of God's Being. It is an aspect of the Word, which in the beginning represented the initiating sound compelling life to take form. It pervades the whole universe.

The OM releases the soul from glamour and enchantment. It is the sound of liberation, the great note of resurrection, of life released from form control. It is the "lost word" which, as it is rediscovered, unveils the glory of the divine self. When we sound the OM we are transmitting the pure life energy of the planetary Logos. The OM is the "lost word" spoken of in the Blue Lodge of Masonry. We now have only a "substitute word" in the Royal Arch. The Masonic tradition has preserved the teaching about the OM, hidden in allegory and ritual.

For aeons the Word of the Soul has been lost but now, through trial and suffering and world tension, it is being rediscovered. The tension of the personality disrupts. The tension of the soul makes entry to the higher evolution possible.

Each of the seven rays has a word of power of its own which, when rightly sounded, with the use of the spiritual will, has a threefold effect. It might be called the sacred word of the Lord of the Ray who is as definitely a spiritual entity as is Sanat Kumara. All rays have a will aspect. To-day disciples are being taught the meaning and quality of sound. To dutifully sound the sacred word is not enough. We need to *feel* the meaning of the Word as we are using it. We can use the spiritual will aspect on whatever ray we may be.

The quality of spirituality is love. The quality of divinity is will. The correct sounding of the sacred word uses both. This we all can do, starting with the desire to do so, to which we add knowledge through study.

We hasten the process of evolution by purifying our three bodies. The OM, when sounded with that intent, loosens the coarser matter in the three bodies so that it can be cast off. When used with intense spiritual aspiration it gathers particles of purer matter to replace the matter cast off.

The wise disciple does not seek to negate matter or escape in consciousness from it, for it is as divine as is the soul. Rather he seeks to master it and control it, and neutralise the bad effects which humanity has produced in using it. If the solar Logos stopped sounding the AUM there would be presently no substance for mankind to dwell in and the great experiment would end in failure. We are engaged in escaping the bondage to materiality not in destroying it. We enslaved ourselves and must release ourselves. This we are doing for we are not helpless robots but sparks of the divine Fire of God's life. By this we mean the life of our solar Logos conditioned by our planetary Logos, Sanat Kumara, "in Whom we live and move and have our being". The science of invocation, including the correct use of the sacred word, will be one of the most important achievements of the new Aquarian age.

Our conquest of material nature proceeds at a rapid pace. Our conquest of human nature must keep equal pace else we prolong worldwide misery. Hence the necessity for self-mastery which in practical terms means that the plans and purposes of our souls are more effective in our lives than our strongest desires and our most desperate physical needs. This we exemplify at the fourth initiation.

EDUCATION

The educational world like other departments of human life is facing change. It cannot escape. That our western civilisation has degenerated cannot intelligently be denied. Therefore new thinking is emerging in our schools, some in the faculty, also among students, too little in those who control the institutions. This is, of course, a generalisation. There are many fine, alert trustees and presidents and professors in higher education.

Surely the standards and goals educators now maintain can be improved; the need for such change is imperative and increasingly this change is welcomed. It need not include condemnation of educators unless they cling to the *status quo*.

Right education has more value than economic affluence. More ease, more comforts, more money and more things owned, do not in fact bring a better way if life. This has demonstrated in the United States. Our educators have more responsibility than our money-makers. Wealth need not and many times does not degrade an individual. It need not degrade a nation. But it is not an adequate measure of success.

The not distant future will be in the hands of the youth of today. For what sort of future are we equipping them? Even self-interest should alert our adults. Does our present education teach right life values? If not, who will? Religious influence is weak if not actually failing. Economic success ignores it. Science refuses responsibility. Without better values lived by, selfish greed increases and engulfs us. Our educators are being pushed to accepting the public good as a part of what they teach.

An educated man is still considered an intelligent man, especially if he has a college degree. We have limited education too much to merely acquiring knowledge about an ever-increasing range of facts. We have included some understanding of the knowledge acquired but not nearly enough. Knowledge without ethical standards is inevitably abused. Better understanding of values brings a better civilisation, less crime, less injustice and cruelty, and more wholesome happiness. Understanding must include intelligent application of the factors which help others. It is not intelligent to be overly self-centred.

Applied understanding of knowledge brings wise action. Wisdom is a practical goal for every educated person. Our graduates should include being wise in, their vision, of the good life. Wisdom should be inculcated, inspired and idealised. Let the student find it natural, and not sacrifice, to ask: how can I benefit my day and age? To want the world at least a tiny bit better because I am in it is not being soft, too idealistic or impractical. It should command more respect than much money. If our educators worked for this achievement we could have it in two generations, and practical beginnings of it in less time than that.

High teacher quality is essential. It is impossible to have good education with poor teachers. If the vision of those training and selecting teachers is poor, most teachers will be poor or at least mediocre. The importance of the teacher to our civilisation is known but too often ignored. Teaching should be and can be an honourable profession. Teacher unions grow by selling the idea to the teachers that they can get more for themselves. Better quality teaching is ignored and the teacher becomes just another job holder in the labour market. They value their job for what they can get. Not all of the union teachers are as crude as this but such is the trend and influence of the increasing teacher unions. There are still a majority of teachers not yet unionised who like students and children and are very fine teachers indeed.

If and when teachers need protection it is the duty of those who control our educational system to give them justice and proper working conditions. How many teachers today are suffering from wrong treatment? A first step towards quality teaching is to be very sure that all teachers are rightly treated; second, more careful selection; and third, higher educational goals in which the teachers share.

Continuing worldwide crisis is also continuing worldwide opportunity for constructive change in the life values we live by. That basic changes are needed is obvious.

Our educators have escaped the influence of organised religion and in so doing have thrown out moral values. We have condemned using educational institutions for ideological indoctrination and have refused responsibility for how our students live. Under financial pressure we have submitted to increasing government interference with what we teach. This generalisation is true in a high percentage of our schools but not in all.

Right education involves more than teaching facts and even in that restricted field we have imprisoned ourselves by material facts which are often soon out-dated by our scientists. We have neglected moral values, personal integrity and given our students no guidelines as to how they should use the knowledge given.

Should the motive for going to college be entirely self-interest? If education does not improve our civilisation, is it worth the billions we pay to keep it going? We dare not abandon education, therefore we must improve it.

We need more effective instruction in how to think. Understanding of the facts imparted requires thinking. Without understanding we remain unintelligent and understanding involves application to life experience. Passing examinations in a dozen or more courses in school is obviously not enough. Right education is more than memory training.

The factor that distinguishes man from animals is the power to think. This is the most important characteristic of every individual and of humanity as a whole. We all think less than we think we think. Mostly we simply respond to what our brain cells can register which is limited by our five senses. Thought is not so limited. Three questions remain largely unanswered in our schools. What is thought?

How can we develop it? For what should we use it?

Should we control our thinking or should what we think be controlled by outside influences such as religious doctrine, ideological propaganda, or mere "getting more for me"? Freedom of thought is of the essence of democracy. Our educational system should inspire freedom of thought as the greatest freedom of all.

Thought-leadership is the most needed of all leaderships in this era of world crisis. Education should produce such leaders. Leadership does not result from obeying rules. Our students study what they are told to study and can stay in school only by passing examinations with an arbitrary grade of correctness as to memory of such knowledge as given them. Drop-outs increase and degrees are less valued by society and the business world.

Wisdom is a right goal for education. To be a wise man is more praiseworthy than to have much money, and in fact is more satisfying. Wise men are respected. Much knowledge and right use of knowledge should lead to right life values which must include personal integrity, cooperation, justice and honesty. Education should not ignore these essentials for a decent civilisation.

All true education is a preparation for the future. Young people may be considered as of two kinds, those who live for today and those who live for tomorrow. The latter show up better in almost all respects but we suffer from the false idea that only living for immediate effects today is practical. Researchers going into our present educational system have come up with such striking statements as: "Most of what a student does consists of re-enacting knowledge put together by the last generation about previous generations' efforts"; "We treat the students' minds as storehouses to be filled rather than instruments to be used"; and "The parents' image of the child's future is more important than teaching him to count or to sign his name".

The successful teacher makes study interesting. If not interesting, it is work to be avoided if possible from which cheating is a helpful escape. Study, when harshly enforced, breeds resentment and deceit. Controlling reactions in class and grading papers is not teaching. We need to teach teachers how to teach before we let them teach. Teaching is not a job measurable in value to the teacher by labour union standards. The child is not something to get a living out of. The teacher who is not interested in children is a misfit from the start, downgrading himself and the child, and cheating social welfare.

Education should prepare our students for a useful life. The influence of his years in school should inspire a useful life as a higher goal than competing for money. Being useful is more desirable than being smart. Wisely chosen personal goals lead to a more satisfying life than selfish, greedy, competing goals can ever bring. Self-respect and personal integrity are more valuable to any man than anything he can get without them. Our educational system should not ignore these values.

World unity and world vision have become a must. We can no longer live in mental boxes created by racial and religious prejudices, national sovereignties, ideological allegiances and economic power. Free thinking is essential for humanity's future. This new trend is essentially an educational responsibility.

We are known as Christian people. And yet our American way of life is un-Christian, regardless of church-going and church allegiances, because our standards of values are directly opposite to the teachings of the Christ.

The Christ did not advocate competition but taught co-operation. He did not advocate the getting of all one could for oneself. He taught sharing. His teachings do not tolerate indifference to the suffering of other people and injustice to human beings.

The individual man who ruthlessly gets all he can for himself regardless of the harm to his neighbour, is not a good citizen. He should modify his greed. The same is true of big business. When any great industry is powerful enough to have what it does affect the economic welfare of the nation, those who control become automatically trustees for the general welfare.

Behind all this there are activities which demonstrate the truth of the underlying reality that the heart of humanity is sound, that it is human instinct to be kind and to be generous and to give the other fellow a fair chance.

It is entrenched greed and selfishness which hold us back and this produces the danger of delay of spiritual evolution itself. This needless delay means prolonged misery, degradation and suffering for millions. Our fate may well be determined by how many of us remain in the ranks of the selfish. Under existing world conditions it behoves us to consider carefully what can be done to hasten human progress toward voluntary conformity to what is best for all human beings.

THE NEED FOR WORLD GOODWILL

The question confronting humanity as a whole in this time of crisis is what can we do about God's Plan for man? Shall we increase our fight against evil? That never yet in all history has been successful for all men, although for a short time blocking some particular evil for some men.

Humanity itself is people and includes all people. Our conquest of the physical substance out of which our planet is made has at last produced a worldwide interdependence that necessitates worldwide cooperation. Our allegiance must be to human good *for all*. Individual freedom of every man to get all he can for himself with no restraints against injury to others leads to anarchy and complete lawlessness. Freedom obviously must be limited, but freedom to live by and work for the good of others needs no limiting.

In the new interdependent world, national competition is being forced to give way to cooperation for world good. We condemn dictators who control governments strong enough to oppose us, saying they destroy freedom, and yet at the same time support dictators in small countries if they conform to our capitalist ideology.

Extreme controlling ideologies, including both capitalism and communism, can deny us mental freedom. Powerful military nations can deny our freedom. Totalitarian nations can deny our freedom. Religious dogmatism and claimed authority can deny our freedom. Wrong, competitive greed falsely justifying wrong values to live by can deny our freedom. Individual failure to accept responsibility for the common good can deny our freedom. If in gaining mental power we lose mental freedom, we lose all and God's Plan for man fails because of man himself.

At the end of the Atlantean era, in which humanity developed its emotional nature, we were abusing that power so completely that the entire civilisation was destroyed in the world flood and God's Plan had to begin anew. If the forces of darkness had won the world war the entire achievements of the present Aryan age would have been lost and another new beginning might have become necessary.

The answer now is acceptance of new values to live by arrived at by free minds. The key is enlightened public education. Cramming our youth with what we call knowledge is not enough. Our educators must develop wisdom in our students and inspire them to use that wisdom for the welfare of all men. We must educate for the common good.

Will the present generation of young people who will soon face future world responsibilities be ready? It largely depends on whether they are educated for the world that is coming or the world that is going. Our present education is focussed on every individual being equipped to get all he can for himself.

The question of how much knowledge the public should have about what its elected and appointed servants are doing goes to the heart of the survival of democracy and of human freedom. The appeal to commonsense in solving this problem is itself commonsense. Reasonableness is an indefinite, inexact gauge to public conduct but so is public opinion itself, without which democracy would die. It is legitimate to say than an intelligently informed public opinion is commonsense.

The bland assumption that what our officials are doing must be kept from public knowledge while they are doing it and only final decisions be given to the people is in practice dangerous and not commonsense. Action takes place during the process and is often of immediate effect. Action in particular situations often has disastrous effects on later events, as for example, Tonkin Bay. That the United States was led into the Vietnam war by stealth is a fact.

The perpetuation of unlimited national sovereignty is a threat to the freedom of all humanity, illustrating the abuse by the part of the welfare of the whole. But we are rapidly learning that all humanity is a unit, that we are in fact one family, and that the welfare of all transcends the privilege of any nation to do as it pleases.

As individuals in democracies we give up certain rights under law to do as we please and know full well that freedom is subject to decent living standards. Whatever undermines the essentials of a decent society must be controlled for the common good but by voluntary consent of man himself, not by dictatorship or indoctrination for any ideology or for the perpetuation of power in the hands of controllers of government in non-dictator nations.

Huge corporations threaten freedom if they do not accept responsibility for public welfare as an essential business policy. Religious organisations claiming divine authority have in the past dictated man's behaviour to an extreme degree so destroying freedom but today have largely lost that power.

Among the many freedoms are the right to travel, the right of free flow of ideas, and freedom of choice. The United Nations Commission on Human Rights is of transcendent importance because it deals with all aspects of freedom.

National separative ambitions remain a threat to freedom. Military control dominating our civilisation characterises our way of international life. Unbridled greed prevents right human relations. We are learning that whatever any man or nation gets at the expense of another is unjustified and that without right human relations life is a cruel fight and freedom is lost. We are coming to recognise that there is no safety except through cooperation, sharing and service to others.

The trend of world events is rapidly submerging the individual in the needs of other human beings on a worldwide scale and this is now being applied as well to nations. National sovereignty is going the same way as private rights have gone, and will doubtless go further in the days to come. No man can live unto himself alone and neither can a nation so live today. Privately-owned land is now held to be a part of national resources. The fight is on to prevent private, corporate and even national ownership of land under the deep sea. Group good is recognised as superior to individual privilege.

The greatest achievement of any world leader, and the greatest gift to humanity any nation can bring at this time, is the end of the cold war, with accompanying disarmament. We could have had this long before now if we had dared to trust and sincerely wanted to cooperate. How much do you and I really want to cooperate with any non-capitalistic nation?

We are being forced to reconsider the realities of the values of the intangibles in international affairs. These basic values are not measurable by inspections, but are so practical and so real that our refusal to trust in their potency leaves us torn and afraid. It becomes clear, therefore, that whatever destroys mutual trust and confidence cuts at the very roots of the possibility of a peaceful world and a decent way of life for our children. We constantly use propaganda on our citizens to keep ourselves convinced that we are too smart to be trustful, and that it is not possible to trust without being foolish. This is simply not true. There are degrees of trustfulness: some foolish, some reasonable, some wise, some obviously the lesser of two evils. We take chances in brinkmanship and in ordinary international diplomacy all the time.

We can, however, recognise a rising tide of appreciation of the essential values of unselfish sharing for the good of humanity, of cooperation with other nations and races, and with the practical demonstration of the usefulness and power of goodwill. We are learning that these are the factors which are essential to the establishing of any improvement in right human relations among the peoples of the world. Right relations is the ultimate necessity and therefore a true goal. It cannot be measured by any electric computer. It cannot be created in any atomic pile. It cannot be monopolised for the benefit of the selfish individual or nation for when so treated it vanishes. Goodwill is the active principle of peace for all men everywhere in the world.

As our global consciousness increases and we recognise that we, as individuals, are a part of one worldwide human family, we accept the fact that there is a divine Plan for man and, as the human race as a whole matures, we accept more responsibility for that Plan. The age of acceptance of imposed authority has ended and the end of the twentieth century finds man as of the age of twenty-one years. Also, the human family is more intelligent and the misuse of mental power has become too dangerous to tolerate. Our need is not for more mental power but to harness that power to wise use for the benefit of all men everywhere in the world. As this is achieved, right human relations will inevitably emerge resulting in peace on Earth.

It is good, therefore, to ponder on God's Plan for man and to increase our own will-to-good, so that as men and women of goodwill we do something about it. As we participate, God's Plan becomes our plan, and for this the Christ has long waited. The need today is for more intelligent cooperators.

Men and Women of Goodwill Everywhere in the World are Called

To RECOGNISE the power of goodwill as a vital force, moulding men's opinions and guiding their actions in constructive cooperation.

To REALISE that this power is greatly needed in world affairs at this time, and that without goodwill among men no lasting peace is possible.

To STRIVE to exemplify goodwill increasingly in their daily lives and so become effective goodwill units within the body of humanity.

To GIVE personal recognition and support to every statement and effort by prominent men and leaders of thought everywhere which has the quality of goodwill, so that whenever and wherever the power of goodwill is used it will have the support of an enlightened public.

To USE their time, their thought and their money to increase goodwill action everywhere in the world.

Men and women of goodwill are those of all countries, all races and of every class who are naturally kind, who prefer friendly relations with others, who know the practical value of unselfishness, and who live constructively. They prefer to understand and to cooperate with other races, nations and individuals. They therefore do not hate, criticise, condemn, attack or destroy. They are intelligent people whose minds have not stifled the dictates of their hearts. They are known by the way they live.

VALUES TO LIVE BY

by Mary Bailey

*The fate of men and nations is determined
by the values which govern their decisions.*

The major problems we face in this changing world are identifiable. The means of solving them are not so obvious but they exist.

The enormously increased scientific and technological knowledge acquired during this century has placed in our hands the means of providing for the physical needs and well-being of the whole human race. Instead we have misused and abused the good earth and its bounty. We have chosen to apply our knowledge to the self-interests and the military and economic world dominance of a small but powerful minority of already over-privileged and highly developed peoples. This imbalance and injustice create new problems while they perpetuate old ones. In spite of abundant natural resources in the world, in spite of man's present ability to increase and develop those resources, poverty and starvation continue for two-thirds of the human race. Millions are destitute, ignorant, homeless or ill-housed; suspicion, warlike postures and weapons development accelerate among the few powerful, industrialised nations of the world; and national self-interest continues to dictate international policies.

Yet it is all a matter of choice. If we so choose we have the genius, the imagination, and the know-how, as well as the resources, to improve the quality of life for all humanity. Therefore, our major problem is one of what we desire and how we decide. It is a problem of character and values. It concerns the goals and objectives we set for ourselves in a world which is one in the essential nature and energy of life itself, one in the destiny we share as a kingdom in nature, and one in the interdependence and interaction of all aspects of life on a planet which is physically one. Because our world crises today do derive basically from whatever values we choose to live by, their solutions can best be identified in terms of value and principle.

Man has distinguished himself for centuries by his selfishness, greed and aggression, and nations by their nationalism, sovereignty and self-interest. These character defects, plus fear and suspicion based on a primitive instinct for survival and self-perpetuation, have accounted for his warlike tendencies. So we have fear, greed and selfishness as the basis of all violence and aggression, on a local, national and international scale, aggravated during the course of this century by materialism. The manufacture, sale and use of death dealing armaments is a massive industry earning huge profits and wielding political power and influence. It has crippled our ability and stifled our will to feed, clothe, house, educate and train the needy. So interwoven with national economies and the political and social structure has this monstrous cancer become, that it successfully resists all direct efforts to control and reduce it to a proportion which more equitably reflects its actual value in defense to any nation.

Therefore, since the structure itself is impregnable, we need to pay attention to the human attitudes of mind and heart which are responsible for the creation and maintenance of all forms of life, ideologies and national goals included. It is human attitudes which determine the quality of life, the accepted values and standards for living, and the decisions and choices which provide for growth and progress or which preserve and perpetuate the *status quo*.

Attitudes of mind and heart can change; and changed attitudes always precede change and growth in any individual or in any race, group or nation of peoples. These attitudes are the consciousness factor; they reflect the principles and ideals accepted as a basis for living. A time of ferment such as today is indicative of profound change in consciousness. It implies a rejection of ideals and attitudes no longer acceptable as a measure of the good life; and it permits entry to ideas more commensurate with the needs and the facts of today's world.

So the principles which should control a new world order for all mankind can emerge with clarity and have great influence on human consciousness. They can impact human hearts and minds, crystallising into attitudes and behaviour with a consequent practical effect on daily life. We might define some of these principles and ideals in these terms:

1. The separateness which has characterised human life on Earth for thousands of years can yield today in this interrelated world structure to attitudes of *inclusiveness, right relationships and goodwill* among men and between nations, leading to peace on Earth.

2. The selfishness and self-interest which have determined our struggle for survival, for identity and supremacy, can be superseded by *selflessness,* the sacrifice of self in the interests of the greater whole. The *will to love* and the *will to serve* the common good reflect the *principle of cooperation* which is the antithesis of competitive self-interest.

3. The materialism of twentieth century man with his capacity to produce material things can be transcended by realisation that *quality* in daily life is more conducive to a good and happy life than quantity. A quality life is dependent on *a spiritual scale of values*—ethical and moral conduct, integrity, honesty, caring and sharing, concern and commitment in practical activities to group good. What is good for all is good for each one.

4. Society and international relationships have long been characterised by irresponsibility. Acting only in its own interests, demanding its own rights and freedoms and ignoring the rights of others, each has created a threat to human survival. An ignorant disregard of the delicate balance existing between all kingdoms in nature has placed the whole planetary ecological system in jeopardy. Responsible behaviour is the only redress. Each individual and every

organised human institution carries a *personal responsibility* for the immediate environment and for the world of which we are all integral parts. The acceptance of personal responsibility in small and large issues sets an infectious and irresistible example.

5. With human society in its present condition of breaking down prior to rebuilding, reactionary cynicism is a familiar attitude of mind, destructive in its effects. Man is, however, a spiritual as well as a material being. In his innate nature he is essentially divine and the evolutionary process consists of his growing awareness of that fact. He has the capacity for knowledge, love and compassion and the ability to organise these capacities for specific aims. He is, therefore, always capable of better attitudes and behaviour and a more active demonstration of his spiritual potential. *A belief in man as an inherently spiritual being and confidence that the heart of humanity is sound provide an incentive and a value to life that inspire constructive attitudes and actions.*

Here, therefore, are five values that men can choose to live by:

> (1) Inclusiveness.
> (2) Selflessness.
> (3) Spiritual quality.
> (4) Personal responsibility.
> (5) Belief in man's potential goodness.

These are simple. They are practical as well as idealistic. Sincerely understood, accepted and practiced by individuals in all walks of life, in all societies, in all nations, the quality and way of life of that society and that nation will change. Groups and nations consist of the individuals that comprise them. The quality of the people and the values they choose to live by determine the quality of the national life and of every kind of leadership; they determine the establishment of policies; the economic priorities; and the social and national objectives. In these concerns, all are involved.

Right constructive values to live by are a practical means of producing a quality way of life for the race of men.

EPILOGUE

Problems of Discipleship Group Service

I should like to share with you some of the rich heritage which has been mine because of the many years of close companionship in service with Alice A. Bailey.

From time to time a disciple emerges into incarnation from one of the ashrams of the Masters with a definite life program which is in harmony with hierarchical purpose and a contribution to that ashram from which the disciple comes. Such a one was Alice A. Bailey. Such a disciple looks above and helps below but, in the Piscean era, very seldom could look across on a level to companionship of understanding and a sharing of the load at that high discipleship level.

Alice's personal life mission as a disciple was to create what we now describe as a pioneering, Aquarian discipleship system of training in the western world. Her personal karma determined place of birth, nationality, family background, social status, etc., which in the end had to be transcended. It inevitably included certain associates with whom she had worked before who were drawn back to her this life. It also involved the steady making of new associates who were attracted by the spiritual note she sounded but more often by purely personality factors.

Alice did thirty years' work and I was with her from the beginning and helped her all the way as best I could. Others came and went. A few here and there stayed through the years. She started destitute with three little girls to take care of and in very poor health. She was stripped in every personality and worldly sense and well-nigh crushed. Under those circumstances the potency of her own soul and the driving force of the plan and purpose of her life emerged triumphant. She fulfilled her obligations to her own Master K.H., and others which she had taken on with his approval, and to the Master D.K. This, however, did not enable her to escape suffering nor did she attempt to so escape.

She was an unusually clear thinker. In the early days when I first knew her, her great driving urge was to know, to understand the ancient wisdom, to pierce through and catch more of the vision, to know more clearly what the Masters wanted.

She had a heritage of fear. This was physical plane fear and might be called a hangover from tragedy in the last life. She did not fear mentally nor was she afflicted with doubts and hesitancies which so befog and confuse many disciples along the way. At the end she emerged with a new emotional equipment which was freed from these fears and she had so perfected her etheric mechanism that all the centres were in full harmonious activity. Hers was a triumphant life.

She carried on in true spiritual fullness the tradition of the succession of disciples of which she was rightfully a part. The first ray quality of her personality was so successfully harnessed to the second ray qualities coming to her from her own soul and carrying into her life the potencies of the Master K.H.'s ashram that through all the years she remained steadfast. I know of no time in the thirty years during which I was her close personal companion, twenty-four hours a day, when she faltered, either in basic purpose or the will to carry on at all costs.

She hesitated at times when confronted with choices of action which might or might not work out very well. She was forced to make decisions about her co-workers which hurt her deeply and which outwardly were very hard to understand by those who do not appreciate discipleship responsibility for group integrity and group usefulness.

Alice endeavoured strenuously to find the right way to bring into the group something of the new Aquarian group responsibility and relationship which is essential for the future in all hierarchical spiritual work and which is a dim reflection of the group relationships and responsibilities within the Master's ashram. She relied on the subjective magnetic attractive power of right discipleship quality.

She conducted her school—the Arcane School—and all of her other activities on the true hierarchical basis and not on the democratic basis. Very early in the history of the school, only a few years after its inauguration, one of the questions asked all students was with regard to this problem of democratic versus hierarchical systems of human relationships. The new age discipleship training schools will naturally be patterned on the ashrams in the Hierarchy.

Her school was founded here in the western hemisphere in the City of New York with the advantage of the talismanic potency which H.P.B. used in this city and in line with the spiritual destiny of the United States towards which the nation is struggling.

Alice was a brilliant and effective public speaker and her platform work all over the world was always used for the spreading of the spiritual teaching to which it was her destiny to make a contribution. For years I have taken her up and down the land in many countries, arranged her lecture tours, secured the financing and done all the rest of it. I have watched her take the platform sometimes a very sick woman and often facing an audience who were very nice people but spiritually rather dumb, and found her talking about spiritual values, human relationships, the Hierarchy, the new group of world servers and many other things without ever mentioning her own books or her own school, the Arcane School.

This, to many who felt themselves more practical minded, seemed very foolish and she was taken to task for it. But she felt that these books were not her books and that they had their own destiny and that a high percentage of their teaching was not going to find very practical expression in her generation.

And as for the school, she sought to create a truly esoteric group. She knew that such a school could not legitimately advertise its wares and would attract entirely the wrong material were it to resort to various more subtle and sometimes tempting processes of bringing in more students.

Her vision of the school was that it was destined always to be, relatively speaking, small in numbers as compared to many of the organised activities in the esoteric field which were in existence at the time she was doing her work, most of which were slowly drying up. She recognised clearly the various stages of training on the Path from the first beginnings of individual recognition of spiritual values on through the Probationary Path, leading ultimately to that type of individual unfoldment which gave the soul sufficient control of the life so that true discipleship could emerge.

She was and is a disciple of high status in the Master's ashram and her function at that time was to help people to become disciples. This process of becoming a disciple can only successfully take place after the Probationary Path has been trodden and its often rather glamourous visions, the spiritual ambitions of the neophyte for personal progress, and the insistent demand that the spiritual teaching and the spiritual teacher should conform to what the probationer's personality liked and wanted, had all grown stale. The quest of the soul must have gained a new grip on the life and so inaugurated a new spiritual dispensation for its shadow, the personality, here on the physical plane.

Without advertising or promotion, people found their way to the Arcane School and if they did, she took them no matter who they were or what their condition seemed to be and gave them their day of opportunity. Often it seemed extremely impractical and gradually as time went on this acceptance of anybody and everybody gave way to a policy involving some selection.

The Arcane School was never run on the basis of what would be pleasing to the students in the school or what they would be more likely to respond to strongly and happily, and never under any circumstances did she permit a distortion of what might be useful to the individual as a disciple because of financial considerations. Over and over again through the years she dropped people who were heavy financial contributors just as readily and just as

quickly as she did anybody else when she came to the con-
clusion that for them the school was not useful.

Alice was very keenly aware of the fact that to build a
school for discipleship training which would carry any of
the pioneering Aquarian influence here in the midst of this
deepest spiritual crisis that humanity has ever yet gone
through, there would have to be a very high standard.

She worked self-sacrificingly, often with the handicap of
great fatigue, for long, heartbreaking hours, perfecting
school courses of study, writing accompanying papers, producing more teaching as the years went by, and so changing and modifying these courses and studies. But in all this
long process the success of her school, as we sometimes
rather unhappily fall into the habit of calling it, was never
her goal. Her goal was to help people go forward on the
Path of Discipleship. The school was a means towards that
end.

All through the years we have recognised, and Alice
specially emphasized, the folly of attempting to hold people
in the school who for one reason or another have come
to us. It is just as foolish as it is to attempt to drag people
into the school, which continually happened in spite of her
reiteration of its uselessness. It was no particular calamity
in her consciousness to lose a student. She knew full well
that in many cases it was very much better for the student
to leave the school and go to another school or go it on
his own for a time.

When she felt that a student was at a struggle point and
that understanding expressed in terms of encouragement
was the needed help, she unhesitatingly gave it. But this
was always from the standpoint of the benefit of the student
and never from the standpoint of the benefit of the school
by keeping him in.

Always Alice insisted that the school should, if properly
conducted, lead to an increasing freedom in the consciousness of those who have been associated with it in discipleship training. This is a matter of that freedom which comes
only when the personality is transcended. Personality de-

mands, likes and dislikes, prejudices, inhibitions, thought habits, etc., must be sufficiently transcended so that detachment in the life can be exemplified without coldness and indifference. Then the influence of the soul in the individual life can really dominate.

We are all enslaved by our emotional nature and by our habitual thought patterns. As personalities we fear being controlled by our souls because we are afraid that it will involve sacrifice and uncomfortable circumstances and giving up things that we as personalities crave and enjoy. The freedom of the disciple is the result of living the life of the soul here in the three worlds and this is the freedom that Alice saw clearly was one of the resulting goals of the life of discipleship usefulness.

It is obvious that there had to come a time when the student had been long enough in the school when he should have a chance to really face this freedom and graduate, so to speak, from the last remnants of the teacher-pupil relationship to the position of spiritual cooperation at the discipleship level in the doing of those things in the world which the Hierarchy wanted done.

This brings us again to the fundamental problem of recognition that the school is not an end in itself but a means to an end, that the assisting of an individual to become a disciple is not in order that *he* achieve that status but so that he can proceed to live and work as a disciple should live and work. This means that he is an active cooperator in the *service* of his fellowmen and that this has become of first importance in his life. He continues to study and he continues to meditate. He continues his companionship with his brothers. But he does this increasingly in the light of his own soul with freedom from the influence of his personality and from the restrictions of those props and guides that were useful at an earlier stage on the Path. The recognition of this necessity and the wisdom of the student in the school graduating into this new age soul freedom does not require any break with the Arcane School by that student unless in the individual case it is desirable for some reason.

The student naturally becomes increasingly a subjective cooperator with the school rather than a student in a school. This is possible because he can find an increasing, constructive companionship and deepened effectiveness in any of the spiritual projects for which the school as a whole has accepted responsibility, such as World Goodwill, Triangles, or Invocation work. Or he can move on in the companionship of many school students to other fields of hierarchical usefulness which are a part of the program of the new group of world servers.

When he consciously takes this step, he is not losing something. He is, in fact, gaining something which is of far greater value than anything he ever heretofore received from the school. He can love the school just as much. He can be of just as much use to the school. He can continue to aid it in many ways. He can support it with his thought and understanding and cooperative action and with his time and with his money, but he should do all this in a new relationship.

In ten short years the note Alice sounded was sufficiently clear and true to pattern and powerful enough so that the group of students in the school were available to be used by the Hierarchy. Such was the need in the world and so eager were those greater than ourselves to find focal points through which hierarchical influence could be spread that her group was used most definitely and almost prematurely. Thus it came about that full advantage was taken of her unique and extraordinary mental vehicle and her telepathic capacity in her etheric brain to set in motion certain activities which had in them the seeds of great spiritual usefulness.

She then became confronted with a threefold responsibility: *first,* for right discipleship training; *second,* for the production and the insuring of the availability of the teaching, which was her thirty-year task (entirely in addition to the Arcane School) with the Master D.K.; and *third,* an emerging group usefulness as a discipleship group in the world in terms of practical influence among the sons of men. Few, indeed, have ever understood the terrific pressure and the overwhelming drive necessary for such a threefold task.

Spiritual self-sufficiency and spiritual pride, complacency and superiorities, are subtle poisons in the disciple's life. They have long been so recognised and a cult of humility has emerged as a sort of cloak which most spiritual workers put on as a virtue. Like every other virtue, our understanding of it is distorted and our application of it often faulty. In certain lives many young disciples achieve most of their results by being spiritually almost arrogant and excessively conscious of their own fancied extreme value. Others not escaping from the habitual belittlement of themselves never succeed in wielding power which they could wield if they were adequately to meet opportunities thrust upon them and achieve results which might have been possible without this defect. Like all the other virtues that the disciple must demonstrate in action, this basic attitude to himself and his life and his work involves a hairline of constant discrimination; and mistakes are made, first one side of the true line and then the other. Disciples are human beings. They are constantly under excessive strain. They are battling through to mastery on all three levels of the personality at once. The fact that they carry spiritual potency elevates them in the eyes of some and brings them drastic and sometimes cruel condemnation from others. These factors among the students and the struggles that inevitably go with them were almost the daily lot of Alice Bailey.

We have left the Piscean age of some 2,200 years behind us and already as a human group have begun to respond to the influence of the Aquarian age. In the Piscean era the sixth ray was dominant with its characteristic of sectarianism. The folly of sectarianism, particularly with relation to the teachings of Djwhal Khul, has been pointed out to us many times but it is a subtle influence and creeps in on us often unrecognised. If we as a group fall victim to it, we will greatly cut down our usefulness, and without usefulness we cannot successfully enter the new age. Alice always insisted that D.K. was not to be used as an authority and that the Arcane School must not become just another sect.

Sectarianism is of the essence of separateness, the greatest heresy of them all, and is the antithesis of togetherness which is one of the main characteristics of the Aquarian type of individual quality. Alice was well aware of this danger, as also was the Tibetan. Alice left many an audience gasping by saying at the close of her lecture: "Do not accept what I tell you today because I say it. I may come back next year and tell you something different". So also D.K. will be teaching something different in the new age.

Through the years I have found the teaching of the Tibetan so amazingly true and right that I hardly know how to escape sectarianism, in spite of his request that we should. How often in a discussion of some part of his teaching someone has come up with a germane quotation and *all thinking stops*. Now we have the answer. That makes us feel good. Instead of presenting a spiritual concept for consideration as a reasonable idea, it is much easier just to tell them what D.K. said. In effect we present him as an authority which is the old age system of training. He has asked us not to do this.

Alice sought always to avoid devoteeism. Yet, in spite of that there were many who were a little unbalanced in their appreciation of her and therefore demonstrated old age Piscean devoteeism in a way which distressed her.

Alice found through the hard school of experience how difficult it is to bring together the necessary material for a headquarters group for a discipleship school. It was apparent to us that it was absolutely essential to create such a group if we were going to meet the need that was increasingly pressing upon us. The work that she did lecturing, through her books, and in her constant and ceaseless interviews with all sorts of people, as it is set forth in her *Unfinished Autobiography,* led to a steady stream of applicants for systematised study. She could not possibly do it all herself. She was faced with the hard task of perfecting a group of cooperators. Otherwise we would have been compelled to fall into the standardised old age patterns.

The system which was evolved was the use of senior students in the school to help new students and the building up of a group of student secretaries. This has become through the years one of the most successful methods of work in the esoteric field. The relationship of the student to the secretary to whom he has been assigned by headquarters, the relationship of the student at the same time to headquarters, and the relationship of the secretary to headquarters, involved many permutations of spiritual influence.

The one outstanding essential feature of this system can be very briefly, although not very adequately, summed up in the statement that in a probationary path school for aspirants the teacher and the school cooperate with the personalities that come into the school; whereas, in a school for discipleship training, the leader of the school, the people at the headquarters of such a school, and so far as it is humanly possible the student secretaries handling students, must cooperate as souls with the souls of the students. Alice Bailey could do this.

After the world war we rebuilt the outer activities of the school and reinaugurated the service activity work. On the continent of Europe, the whole structure had been wrecked. We now find ourselves faced with a new world, with humanity purged of the heavy karma of much of its previous folly, struggling desperately to shake off the old age influences and bring in a new era of sharing, cooperation and right human relations. These ideas are very familiar to us but the world struggle is still going on between old age materialistic nationalism and new age world interdependence and sharing.

ESOTERIC TRAINING

Training for new age discipleship is provided by the *Arcane School*. The principles of the Ageless Wisdom are presented through esoteric meditation, study and service as a way of life.

Write to the publishers for information.

World Goodwill is offering a study course on the six main problems of humanity. The problems dealt with are:

> The Psychological Renewal of the Nations
>
> The Problem of Education
>
> The Problem of Capital, Labour and Employment
>
> The Problem of the Racial Minorities
>
> The Problem of the Churches
>
> The Problem of International Unity.

There is no charge for the course, but contributions are received for actual administrative expense.

Write to the publishers for information about this course.

Esoteric Teaching on the Air. An intensification in the work of making the teachings available on public radio was inaugurated by Lucis Trust in 1974. A variety of radio programs are in use today "conditioning the minds and hearts of men for the reappearance of the Christ". Emphasising the basic values and principles of discipleship living, the effectiveness of the teachings on radio is already becoming apparent in many parts of the world.

Broadcasting material and information are available on request from Radio Lucis, 866 United Nations Plaza, New York, New York 10017.

PART II

MANTRAMS
ancient and modern

Compiled from the writings of
DJWHAL KHUL

with commentary by
FOSTER BAILEY

Section I

FOREWORD

"Mantric forms are phrases, words and sounds which by virtue of rhythmic effect achieve results that would not be possible apart from them". For best effect they should be sounded on their right musical note. This requires a degree of soul consciousness. Ideally the soul and the personality use the mantram simultaneously in perfect harmony.

An aspirant uses a mantram as an affirmation in which he has faith. The effect is often mostly the result of the power of the words of the mantram, but it is possible to invoke the action of the soul before developing the ability to register soul action. Faith is also powerful even in little-evolved man, and the use of mantrams is very ancient.

Thirty-five mantrams were brought to this planet by "The Lords of the Flame from Venus for use by the Hierarchy". They are used to inaugurate planetary events and unlock the mysteries of the subplanes of the five planes of human evolution. They exist in Sensa and Sanskrit. Certain threefold mantric words are constantly sounded forth by the solar Logos, the Heavenly Man, the Monad and the Ego. The wider the field contacted the more powerful the mantram used.

A mantram, when correctly sounded, creates a vacuum in matter between the disciple and his Master resembling a funnel. Once a year the entire Hierarchy employs a mantram that creates a unifying vacuum channel between all hierarchical members and also extends, via Sanat Kumara, to the solar Logos. This is a supreme moment of spiritual effort and vitalisation.

Certain mantrams are given to candidates for major initiations and pronounced by the initiator on those occasions. Later, when humanity is sufficiently harmless to consciously cooperate with the devas, appropriate mantrams will be used. Mantrams calling a healing or a protective deva are known to few disciples. An accepted disciple of a certain grade is given a mantram which calls the attention of his Master. This can be used for protection or for spiritual work entrusted to the disciple by his Master. The use of hierarchical mantric words "destroys the germs of evil thus strengthening the life found in every form". It thereby purifies the forms being used by the life and hastens the evolutionary life of humanity.

Certain mantrams have direct effect on some one of the three vehicles, physical, emotional or mental. Such mantrams, often so distorted as to be practically useless, are used in the religious services of religions all over the world.

Each of the seven rays has its own mantric formulas and mantric sounds which are available in meditation at a certain stage in evolution. They link the disciple with his soul, put him in contact with his Master and link him with his own egoic group.

There are special mantrams for healing and for the development of certain psychic powers for use in service, and also mantrams which have a direct effect on the force centres in both the physical and emotional bodies. The mantram "*Om mani padme hum*" is one of the most sacred of all the eastern mantrams. Each syllable has a secret meaning which produces seven different results.

There are mantrams based entirely on the Sacred Word. These are of great power and when the power of sound is more perfectly understood they will be widely used in the Occident. The use of sound in spiritual work is as yet an undeveloped art.

The more we contemplate the use of mantrams the more we realise that they are a basic technique in the entire evolutionary process, their usefulness extending far beyond the human kingdom on one planet. It seems sure that the use of mantrams by humanity will increase and be more effective in the new Aquarian age. We can therefore increase our use of mantrams now as a service to our fellow-men. It is an ever ready tool available to all. We may well study it and practice it.

MANTRAMS
with commentary

The Great Invocation

From the point of Light within the Mind of
God
    Let light stream forth into the minds of
      men.
        Let Light descend on Earth.

From the point of Love within the Heart of
God
    Let love stream forth into the hearts of
      men.
        May Christ return to Earth.

From the centre where the Will of God is
known
    Let purpose guide the little wills of
      men—
        The purpose which the Masters
        know and serve.

From the centre which we call the race of
men
    Let the Plan of Love and Light work out
     And may it seal the door where evil
      dwells.

Let Light and Love and Power restore the
Plan on Earth.

The Great Invocation

The Great Invocation is a mantram of great power carrying all the seven ray energies. The now rapidly increasing energy of the seventh ray implements and increases the effectiveness of the first and second ray energies as they flow into and through humanity. The combined potency of these three ray energies neutralises the destructive effects of the misuse by humanity of the third ray energy and increases the effects of its right use. This also applies to the effects of the right and wrong use of the fifth ray, so that all six rays ultimately make the triumph of the fourth ray inevitable.

The Great Invocation was preceded by two preliminary stanzas. The first, issued in 1935, was immediately successful, producing an area of peace and quiet on the astral plane. It was used by a comparatively few people but its effect was preserved by the Hierarchy and its use by humanity discontinued. Its wording was as follows:

Let the Forces of Light bring illumination to mankind.

Let the Spirit of Peace be spread abroad.

May men of goodwill everywhere meet in a spirit of cooperation.

May forgiveness on the part of all men be the keynote at this time.

Let power attend the efforts of the Great Ones.

So let it be, and help us to do our part.

The second stanza, issued in 1940, was an hierarchical
test, "a decision point in time of crisis". Its wording was as
follows:

Let the Lords of Liberation issue forth.
> Let Them bring succour to the sons of men.
> Let the Rider from the Secret Place come forth,
> And coming, save.
> Come forth, O Mighty One.

> Let the souls of men awaken to the Light,
> And may they stand with massed intent.
> Let the fiat of the Lord go forth:
> The end of woe has come!
> Come forth, O Mighty One.
> The hour of service of the saving force has now
> arrived.
> Let it be spread abroad, O Mighty One.

> Let Light and Love and Power and Death
> Fulfill the purpose of the Coming One.
> The WILL to save is here.
> The LOVE to carry forth the work is widely spread
> abroad.
> The ACTIVE AID of all who know the truth is also
> here.
> Come forth, O Mighty One, and blend these three.
> Construct a great defending wall.
> The rule of evil *now* must end.

(Front matter in *The Externalisation of the Hierarchy*)

The third stanza of the Great Invocation was given out in 1945 and is used by all men everywhere in the world.

> From the point of Light within the Mind of God
>   Let light stream forth into the minds of men.
>   Let Light descend on Earth.

> From the point of Love within the Heart of God
>   Let love stream forth into the hearts of men.
>   May Christ return to Earth.

> From the centre where the Will of God is known
>   Let purpose guide the little wills of men—
>   The purpose which the Masters know and serve.

> From the centre which we call the race of men
>   Let the Plan of Love and Light work out
>   And may it seal the door where evil dwells.

Let Light and Love and Power restore the Plan on Earth.

The Great Invocation is unique as a world prayer in that it asks nothing for the separated self. Heretofore only advanced initiates and disciples could use such an invocation because only such people could voice and carry that high vibration of pure selflessness. That the masses of men in this new age will use it is eloquent evidence that God's Plan for man is succeeding and that the human kingdom is evolving according to that Plan. This is possible because "the heart of humanity is sound", and God dwells therein. This Invocation as it unfolds in our consciousness by daily use, voices the destiny and Plan for man for the new Aquarian age. Let us consider it stanza by stanza.

From the point of Light within the Mind of God, let light stream forth into the minds of men. Let Light descend on Earth.

Among the many qualities of the human soul, *light* and *love* and *power* are transcendent. The Great Invocation invokes *Light* for all men everywhere in the world regardless of their stage of evolution, their intelligence or lack of it, whether or not they live clean or sinful lives or whatever their circumstances may be. It is not selective for the chosen few. The Christ shuts the door on no one. This Invocation cannot be used effectively for the benefit of the individual man. The user benefits only as all men benefit. But we can remember that those who cooperate with the Christ evolve faster than those who do not.

A key word for the Great Invocation is *cooperate,* not merely follow. The Christ uses the Great Invocation to hasten God's Plan and to evoke spiritual potency for his work and when we rightly use the Great Invocation we are cooperating with him. In the new age the door stands wide open for all to cooperate in God's Plan and with the Christ. "And God said, Let there be light, and there was light", and so the worlds were made and the power of "the Word" was released.

From the point of Love within the Heart of God, let love stream forth into the hearts of men. May Christ return to Earth.

Love is the greatest thing in the world. This the Mystery Schools of all ages have taught. This teaching is the foundation of all the values to be found in modern esotericism in the West today. Christ came some 2,000 years ago and another new religion emerged. It is in fact a religion of love. He taught that God was a God of love, likened unto a loving Father. A loving Father does not send his children to everlasting torture in a man-created hell. There is no such place.

The new age, aided by the Christ and all of us who so choose, will produce a new religion. That it will be a religion made possible by love we may be sure. Love cannot be superseded. Once released in the hearts of men it never dies. Therefore, we invoke love from the heart of God to stream into the hearts of men, and many there be whose hearts are now closed to God's love. The need for love is great.

From the centre where the Will of God is known, let purpose guide the little wills of men—the purpose which the Masters know and serve.

We note that the Masters are proclaimed, not the Master. This is important because it refers to the occult Hierarchy of the planet. Therefore, we are enjoined to make known the existence of the Hierarchy and to do so not on authority but in acceptable, reasonable terms.

The Great Invocation invokes the will of God which is the manifestation of His purpose in all His creations. We are now taught that the recognition of the spiritual will and its conscious use by man is a next great step forward for the human family. It may well be the greatest new note of the new age religion. This spiritual will is the expression of the purpose of love itself. Light, love and power, as invoked by this new world mantram, are in perfect harmony. They are the manifested use by God of all the ray forces in His work of creation.

From the centre which we call the race of men, let the Plan of Love and Light work out, and may it seal the door where evil dwells.

The power of the Great Invocation is focussed in the human kingdom, partly for the benefit of man, but much more for the benefit of all the other kingdoms. It is so powerful and cuts so deep that it can make this Earth a "sacred planet" and so a constructive asset in the solar system, which it is not now.

It is man's destiny to resolve the problem of good and evil on this planet. What we call evil is only evil for us because of our violation of God's law with relation to it. What we call evil is part of God's life and cannot be destroyed. That force now functions in the human family because we let it in. It does not belong here. We let it in and we must put it out. It has its own rightful place where it has a constructive function. Our ideas about good and evil are indeed inadeqate. We need new thinking here.

Therefore, in the Great Invocation we have God's Plan worked out by man closing the door where evil dwells.

The divine Plan is a plan of light and love and this Plan must work out in the centre which we call the race of men. So proclaims the Great Invocation and under God's Will *we* must work it out. The success of the purpose of the Lord of the World, Sanat Kumara, awaits our achievement. And it must be our achievement because we are not spiritual robots helpless before a destiny we cannot control.

Let Light and Love and Power restore the Plan on Earth.

A key word in this last stanza is "restore". The ultimate destiny of man requires self-mastery. We were given the right to choose what we would do even to the disrupting and delay of God's Plan, and we did disrupt it. Therefore our suffering is our own doing, not God's, and we now face the accumulated results in the last quarter of the twentieth century. Continued wrong doing can make it much worse but wise action can neutralise much of its worst effects.

Every man who uses the Great Invocation is helping his fellowmen. Every man who brings the Great Invocation to the attention of others is cooperating with the planetary Hierarchy and with the head of that Hierarchy, the Christ.

The Gayatri

O Thou Who givest sustenance to the
universe,

From Whom all things proceed,

To Whom all things return,

Unveil to us the face of the true Spiritual
Sun

Hidden by a disc of golden Light

That we may know the Truth

And do our whole duty

As we journey to Thy sacred feet.

The Gayatri

The Gayatri is one of the oldest mantric prayers humanity has ever had. When even partially understood its potency is very great. To assume that man himself created this prayer would be presumptuous indeed. It came to us from the Hierarchy. The Gayatri is not a desperate cry of humanity for relief. It transcends all that man has achieved through all the ages of his evolution and we are confronted with the realisation that the universe was not created to aid humanity but that humanity was created to aid a cosmic Plan.

The divine purpose of God's Plan for man is not to perfect a human kingdom on this small planet Earth, freed from pain and suffering and living at ease. But humanity has been given the priceless gift of controlling its own destiny and emerging a victor, a glorious goal indeed, an inspiring and soul-stirring goal. That we shall ultimately emerge a victor is inevitable, else this Plan for man would demonstrate a divine failure.

Today we are wallowing in world crisis because of this priceless gift which we have not yet learned how to use. We are responsible for human suffering and misery and must ourselves cure it. This we shall do because the heart of humanity is sound, for every human heart is a manifested bit of God's life.

The Gayatri places our destiny as part of a cosmic Plan, the majesty of which we cannot comprehend. It is a declaration of ultimate victory to be achieved by knowing the truth and doing our whole duty, and this we do as we journey to God's sacred feet. Three great concepts are thus implanted in human consciousness: the quest for truth, the need to do our whole duty, and the fact of evolution itself.

In the Gayatri we pray to the creator of the entire universe and so establish the beginnings of a conscious relationship, transcending all limitations of "the one supreme God". Its use builds into our deepest consciousness the reality that man is God-created and not the mere result of a biological urge.

In the long past ages all we knew about God was what we were told with boundless claims of authority. Those thus gaining power over us proclaimed that religion did not have to be reasonable. In the new Aquarian age we are now entering, the power of the human mind cannot longer be denied, for humanity has come of age and religion will have to be reasonable or it will have no power over us. Man will think more purposefully about God than ever before.

The Gayatri is a prayer for more knowledge about our solar Logos. That so ancient a prayer could have such an objective is deeply significant. Now at long last we are exploring outer space, learning new and amazing things about the solar system in which our little planet Earth has its place. Now the full potency of this ancient prayer can become effective. All men everywhere in the world will gain much as it is increasingly used by the men and women of goodwill. Its use by disciples everywhere will bring new effectiveness to all their work. "The hour of the saving force has now arrived", and the Gayatri is an agent of that saving force. Its day of greatest usefulness has surely come.

The Mantram of
the New Group of World Servers

May the Power of the one Life pour through
the group of all true servers.

May the Love of the one Soul characterise
the lives of all who seek to aid
the Great Ones.

May I fulfill my part in the one Work
through self-forgetfulness,
harmlessness, and right speech.

The Mantram of the New Group of World Servers

A strong subjective relation exists between all servers of the Plan. This coherent, integrated group is transmitting spiritual energy throughout all areas of human thought and action to strengthen world unity and right human relationships. Men and women of goodwill link up in thought *every day at five o'clock* with this world group of servers, using the following brief dedication, silently and with focussed attention:

> May the Power of the one Life pour through the group of all true servers.
>
> May the Love of the one Soul characterise the lives of all who seek to aid the Great Ones.
>
> May I fulfill my part in the one Work through self-forgetfulness, harmlessness, and right speech.

This can be done in a few seconds of time wherever one may be.

This mantram probes more deeply into the spiritual essentials of progress on the Path by accepted disciples than almost any other mantram we have. Its contemplation and daily use brings in a flood of divine energy. As used by an individual it is a pledge by the personality to the soul. As used by a group it produces group alignment and consecration to world service. It is a direct appeal to God and when sincerely used with firm intent inevitably evokes response. The three required essentials for the world server: *self-forgetfulness, harmlessness,* and *right speech,* cover the entire life expression of a pledged world disciple, a pledge he has taken to his own soul and which he demonstrates as a disciple in the ashram of his Master.

Right speech includes all self-expression of personal thoughts, desires and actions. Harmlessness eventually brings complete freedom from what has been called bad karma. Complete self-forgetfulness is the climax of world discipleship living. In a certain sense it transcends even selflessness. One who is still seeking selflessness has not yet achieved self-forgetfulness. And yet complete selflessness means no more self and the complete freedom of the soul from the necessity to reincarnate again. The closing line of this mantram is of profound, far-reaching significance. When rightly used with knowledge and firm intent, the words are very powerful. They sum up in dynamic first ray potency the way of life of all disciples which leads them eventually to complete mastery of life itself. Selflessness, harmlessness and right speech are here dedicated to the one work of hastening the evolution of spiritual livingness in humanity.

Deep pondering on selflessness reveals many aspects of discipleship living and is an effective key to progress on the Path. Its achievement results in the complete control of the personality by the soul and, therefore, of the final entry into full membership into the Hierarchy.

Selflessness includes more than self-forgetfulness. I as a personality can temporarily forget myself in strenuous action in pursuing my own goal. Selflessness is a quality of the soul. Self-consciousness is lost in group consciousness when at last the great heresy of separateness is overcome. Selflessness is therefore the ultimate goal.

The Mantram of Unification

The sons of men are one and I am one with
them.

I seek to love, not hate;

I seek to serve and not exact due service;

I seek to heal, not hurt.

Let pain bring due reward of light and love.

Let the soul control the outer form, and life
and all events

And bring to light the love that underlies
the happenings of the time.

Let vision come and insight.

Let the future stand revealed.

Let inner union demonstrate and outer
cleavages be gone.

Let love prevail. Let all men love.

The Mantram of Unification

This mantram declares two realities. First, that the user is one with all humanity and second, that humanity as a whole responds to the divine Plan. Five aspects of this Plan are dealt with:

1. The reward of human suffering.
2. The control of human life by the soul.
3. Precipitation of the vision, revealing the future.
4. The demonstration of the inner unity of all humanity.
5. Humanity dominated by love.

Here we have a marvelous summation of the divine Plan for man. To whatever extent we, as individuals, understand it and live by it, we aid the whole of humanity. It brings meaning and purpose to our lives.

This mantram is a source of strength for all disciples active in spiritual work.

Joy

Joy settles within the heart

But has winged its way from the secret
place within the head.

I am that bird of joy,

Therefore with joy I serve.

Joy

D.K. says, "Joy results from a blending of power, will and strength with love, wisdom and skill in action and speech". It is much more than a pleasant sensation. It is a precipitation of an aspect of the life of the human soul into the life of the personality and a combining with it. It carries specific energies which can be identified and cultivated. It is magnetic and attractive and helps all who contact it. It heals and protects because it harmonises and creates a positive condition. Worry cannot endure and fear vanishes in its presence. It transcends prejudices and petty pride. It is acceptable to everybody, arouses no resentment and kills jealousy. It produces confidence and poise. It increases the effectiveness of every world server. It can be developed in oneself by pondering upon it. Recognising its value opens the door to acquiring it. To be effective, it must be real, not a pose to get something. True joy is quiet and evidences an inner peace.

Ancient Mantram

Lead me from darkness to Light,

from the unreal to the Real,

from death to Immortality.

Ancient Mantram

This statment is one of the oldest mantric prayers known to man. It is in worldwide use by Freemasons, not as a mantram, but in connection with action in the Blue Lodge.

It can, however, be used as a mantram because it invokes three fundamental qualities essential for individual progress on the path of human evolution.

The darkness referred to is the primitive condition of the undeveloped human mind.

The reality referred to is occultly understood as the fact of the divine Plan for humanity on this planet, Earth. To know this Plan is to know the reason for life itself. This requires the development of the mind.

The fact that all men are immortal gives meaning and purpose for life. The real man is the soul. After the physical body goes, the soul lives on. Now some men say: *I have a Soul.* In the days to come all men will say: *I am a Soul.*

When rightly used and occultly understood, it is one of the most powerful mantrams we have.

Group Fusion

I am one with my group brothers and all that I have is theirs.

May the love that is in my soul pour forth to them.

May the strength that is in me lift and aid them.

May the thoughts which my soul creates reach and encourage them.

Group Fusion

This mantram voices the essential service which every accepted disciple gives to all his brother disciples. This he gives spontaneously with no thought of loss. It becomes as natural and as constant as breath itself.

When one can say in utter selflessness: "All that I have is theirs", all barriers are gone and complete unity rules. Then comes the most complete sense of freedom we can know. When nothing that we have is ours, then there is nothing left to give but ourselves, and this last gift brings bliss and graduation from the hall of learning in the school of life.

The Affirmation of a Disciple

I am a point of light within a greater Light.

I am a strand of loving energy within the stream of Love divine.

I am a point of sacrificial Fire, focussed within the fiery Will of God.

> And thus I stand.

I am a way by which men may achieve.

I am a source of strength, enabling them to stand.

I am a beam of light, shining upon their way.

> And thus I stand.

And standing thus, revolve

And tread this way the ways of men,

And know the ways of God.

> And thus I stand.

The Affirmation of a Disciple

This affirmation "and thus I stand" is a declaration of a goal. Few there be who now stand as here stated. The Masters in the Hierarchy so stand and we all, if we so choose, can some day thus stand. Meanwhile, we can all legitimately use it as the affirmation of our goal. Its right use opens the door through which we can pass, surprisingly soon, to partial achievement. Its right use requires due humility. Its inspiring call gives wings to our feet and brings in the magic of Mercury. Holding it in our consciousness brings joy in our goal of world discipleship and speeds us on our way.

The first part is the declaration of our soul. The second part is a statement of the program of every world server. The third part is eloquent of being in this world but not of it, evidencing the combined knowledge of the soul and the personality. It reminds us that the personality is not to be crushed but to be used. At the fourth initiation the personality completely surrenders to the soul with no reservations whatsoever.

Those who dare to face the consequences can rightly use this first ray mantram.

Invocation of Light

Radiance we are and power. We stand forever with our hands stretched out, linking the Heavens and the earth, the inner world of meaning and the subtle world of glamour.

We reach into the Light and bring it down to meet the need. We reach into the silent place and bring from thence the gift of understanding. Thus with the Light we work and turn the darkness into day.

Invocation of Light

This mantram "Radiance we are", gives strength and confidence to all world servers. It inspires persistence in discipleship action. The radiance invoked is the light of the soul ever increasing in the aura of the server. The power invoked is the power inherent in every human soul, plus the power of the Christ and the Hierarchy. It should not be used to increase the power of the personality. The energy released is group energy and the use of the pronoun "we" is significant. It is intended for use by groups, not by individuals.

Mantram of Fire

I seek the Way; I yearn to know. Visions I see, and fleeting deep impressions. Behind the Portal, on the other side, lies that which I call home, for the circle has been well-nigh trod, and the end approaches the beginning.

I seek the Way. All ways my feet have trod. The Way of Fire calls me with fierce appeal. Naught in me seeks the way of peace; naught in me yearns for earth.

Let the fire rage, the flames devour; let all the dross be burnt; and let me enter through that Gate, and tread the Way of Fire.

Mantram of Fire

This mantram is one of the most potent we have. When rightly used with understanding and right motive it can bring soul control of the life. Its use can hasten the climax in consciousness of the long series of incarnations in the human family. For the aspirant it will create a conscious link with his Master and so eventually bring him into the Hierarchy.

Other mantrams can help to do the same thing. This they all do in degree because they increase the usefulness of the user in aiding the divine Plan for the whole human kingdom. Without desire to be useful to the Plan we stumble needlessly as we go.

The effects in your life of the use of this mantram will be greater than you will know, but beware of self-induced glamour about results.

Hierarchical Invocation—Meeting Need

I know, O Lord of Life and Love, about the
need.

Touch my heart anew with love,

That I too may love and give.

Hierarchical Invocation—Meeting Need

The *second* aspect of divinity works through mantric combinations. At each incarnation finer forms are required and the mantric formulas grow more complicated. They are finally sounded mentally on the mental plane. When the causal body is completely built and expressing the purpose of the monad, mantrams as we now have them are no longer needed and the monadic sound perpetuates the evolutionary process.

The use of mantrams by man can affect animals beneficially or harmfully. Thus right relations between the human and animal kingdoms can be hastened, a triumph of fourth ray energy.

The white magic of group work can use mantric sound to attract money for spiritual work. In the past, crude forms of mantrams have been used to get money for individuals. Because of developed mental power we can now use mantrams for group purposes.

One of the more recent groups in the Hierarchy for a specific purpose has been called *the financial group*. This group has been an outstanding success, inspiring the use of money for philanthropic work all over the world. Here we have man aiding man, a great spiritual step forward. Now we are entering a new cycle of action by this financial group. There are now enough disciples exemplifying selflessness, harmlessness and right speech so that they can be trusted to use money rightly for spiritual purposes.

We are entering a new age of abundant money for the work of Hierarchy and the Christ. The evil result of misuse of money is one of the main causes of the death of our civilisation. Our continuing world crisis is more and more focussing on economic factors. The door is now wide open for each one of us to cooperate with this new age action by the financial group in Hierarchy.

Section II

MANTRIC VERSES FOR MEDITATION

He who faces the light and stands within its radiance is blinded to the issues of the world of men; he passes on the Lighted Way to the great Centre of Absorption. But he who feels the urge to pass that way, yet loves his brother on the darkened path, revolves upon the pedestal of light and turns the other way.

He faces towards the dark, and then the seven points of light within himself transmit the outward streaming light, and lo! the face of those upon the darkened way receives that light. For them the way is not so dark. Behind the warriors—twixt the light and dark—blazes the light of Hierarchy.

May the Holy Ones, whose disciples we know ourselves to be, show us the light we seek, give us the strong aid of Their compassion and Their wisdom. There is a peace which passeth understanding; it abides in the hearts of those who live in the Eternal. There is a power which maketh all things new; it lives and moves in those who know the Self as One. May that peace brood over us, that power uplift us, till we stand where the One Initiator is invoked, till we see His star shine forth.

I play my part with stern resolve, with earnest aspiration; I look above, I help below; I dream not, nor I rest; I toil; I serve; I reap; I pray; I mount the Cross; I tread the Way; I tread upon the work I do; I mount upon my slain self; I forego peace; I forfeit rest, and in the stress of pain I lose myself and find my Self and enter into peace.

Forgetting the things which lie behind I will strive towards my higher spiritual possibilities. I dedicate myself anew to the service of the Coming One and will do all I can to prepare men's minds and hearts for that event. I have no other life intention.

May the Holy Ones

Whose pupils we aspire to become

So strengthen us that we may give ourselves

Without reserve,

Seeking nothing, asking nothing,

 Hoping nothing for the separated self.

May we be content to be

In the light or in the dark,

To be active or passive,

To work or to wait,

To speak or to be silent,

To take praise or reproach,

To feel sorrow or joy—

Our only wish to be what They need

As instruments for Their mighty work,

And fill whatever post is vacant

In Their household.

In the centre of the will of God I stand.

Naught shall deflect my will from His.

I implement that will by love.

I turn towards the field of service.

I, the Triangle divine, work out that will

Within the square and serve my fellowmen.

In the centre of all love I stand;

From that centre I, the soul, will outward
    move;

From that centre I, the one who serves, will
    work.

May the love of the divine Self be shed
    abroad

In my heart, through my group, and through-
    out the world.

More radiant than the Sun,

Purer than the snow,

Subtler than the ether,

Is the Self, the Spirit within my heart.

I am that Self. That Self am I.

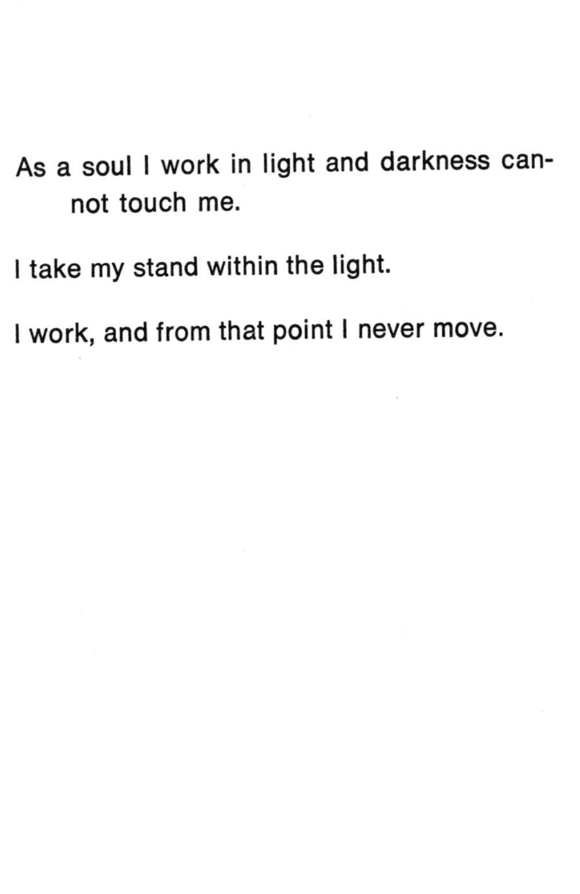

As a soul I work in light and darkness cannot touch me.

I take my stand within the light.

I work, and from that point I never move.